Harvard Health Publications
HARVARD MEDICAL SCHOOL
Trusted advice for a healthier life

MW01014046

Dear Reader,

Years ago, I saw a patient in the beginning stages of dementia. She still had moments of great clarity, and in one of those times she lamented, "I'm vanishing as a person." Her words have stuck with me because they seemed like such a lucid description of the impact of dementia on a person.

In many ways, our memories shape who we are. They make up our internal biographies—the stories we tell ourselves about what we've done with our lives. Our memories tell us who we're connected to, who we've touched during our lives, and who has touched us. In short, our memories are crucial to the essence of who we are as human beings.

Memory loss also affects the practical side of life. Remembering how to get from your house to the grocery store or how to do the tasks that make up your job allows you to take care of your needs. That's what makes dementia so scary—losing your memory means both losing your ability to live independently and not being able to remember your past experiences. It's not surprising, then, that concerns about cognitive decline rank among the top fears people have as they age.

And there's no getting around the fact that the ability to remember does change with age. Many of these changes are normal, and not a sign of dementia. As you'll read about in the section of this report titled "Forgetting: What's normal?" (see page 9), many of these changes increase as the brain ages. Unfortunately, some people have the more serious memory problems associated with dementia. We will review the different forms of dementia, too.

If your memory is still healthy—even if you're forgetting a bit more than you'd like—now's the time to commit to protecting your brain from ill consequences. When it comes to the brain, one key to successful aging is what experts call cognitive reserve, the brain's capacity to withstand damage associated with disease or injury. Although scientists once thought that the adult brain did not grow new brain cells (neurons), we now know that the brain keeps making new cells and connections throughout life. This plasticity, or ability to change, means that you may be able to have an impact on neuronal growth. This report discusses some new research on this subject and gives examples of memory strategies that may help.

Though the connection may not seem obvious at first, keeping the rest of your body healthy is a crucial way to preserve your memory. Many medical conditions—from heart disease to depression—can affect your memory. Staying physically and mentally active turns out to be among the best prescriptions for maintaining a healthy brain and a resilient memory.

Sincerely,

Kirk R. Daffner, MD

Kirk R. Daffner, M.D.
Medical Editor

Dr. Daffner would like to acknowledge Dr. Marilyn Albert and Dr. Aaron Nelson, the previous editors of this Special Health Report, who provided the foundation for the current presentation, and thank the Wimberly family, the Muss family, and the Mortimer/Grubman family for their generous support.

What is memory?

Memory is often used as a catchall phrase referring to a person's general thinking (cognitive) abilities. Actually, memory is just one—albeit very important—aspect of cognition. It refers specifically to all that you remember as well as your capacity for remembering. Not all memories are created equal. Some memories are meant to be retained for a short period and then discarded. For example, you remember the telephone number of the local pizza place only long enough to make the call. But memories that are more important are stored in the brain and can be retrieved at will: the names of close friends and relatives, the multiplication tables, your phone number, and other information you use regularly. Certain kinds of information can be memorized only if you concentrate, whereas other kinds of memories, such as the faces of people you see regularly and the steps of simple everyday routines like brushing your teeth, are absorbed without conscious effort. The process of learning new information, storing it, and recalling it involves a complex interplay of brain functions (see Figure 1).

Researchers and neuroscientists have devised several classification systems to describe the various forms of memory. One major system relies on duration, making a distinction between short-term memories, which are fleeting, and long-term memories, which can persist for a lifetime. Another scheme breaks memories down according to the type of information they contain, such as whether they are straight facts, specific events, or learned procedures for doing something.

Forming and storing a memory is a multistep process that involves several parts of the brain. The memory of an event is not a single entity, like a book on a shelf. Instead, it is the aggregation of multiple streams of sensory information, filtered through the perception of the person observing or participating in the event. Each of the different components of a memory is stored and processed in a different region of the brain. It is not uncommon for a person to have problems with one type of memory, such as recalling specific events, but to function normally in other areas, such as remembering routes to different locations.

Figure 1 Anatomy of memory processing

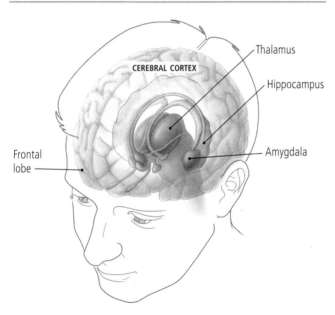

Deep within the brain, a structure known as the hippocampus plays a crucial role in acquiring and consolidating new memories. The nearby amygdala is the part of the brain that reacts to emotionally powerful information, helping the brain retain information that has emotional impact. Once a memory is established (consolidated), it is stored mainly in areas of the cerebral cortex, the large, domed outer layer of the brain.

Short-term memory

This is information that the mind stores temporarily, encompassing what you need to remember in the next few seconds or minutes. Short-term memories include, for example, the name of the person who just spoke at a dinner party (as well as what that person said), and the date and time of the appointment you just made—and must remember only until you write it in your date book.

Working memory is a form of short-term memory that involves actively holding information and manipulating it. For example, working memory comes into play when you remember prices at the supermarket while at the same time performing a computation with them so you can compare costs between different brands or quantities.

Short-term memories are supposed to be fleeting. They turn over at a high rate because new ones are continually replacing them, and there are only so many short-term memories you can keep in mind. Research shows that the average person can hold only about seven (plus or minus two) unrelated "bits" of information in mind at one time. That's why it's easier to remember a seven-digit phone number than a longer number such as the identification number on a driver's license.

The relatively transient nature of your short-term memory is actually beneficial because it allows you to discard unnecessary information. Imagine what life would be like if you kept every short-term memory— the name of the telemarketer who called your house an hour ago, the price of each dish you ordered from a Chinese restaurant, what color tie your friend wore yesterday. Your mind would be so overloaded with trivia that you'd have trouble focusing on the things that really are important. It would be as if you kept all your junk mail and let it bury your personal letters, bank statements, and other important documents.

Short-term memory has another limitation. It's fragile and easily disturbed by interruptions. If you're trying to remember a phone number and someone walks into the room and asks you a question, chances are you'll forget the number and have to look it up again. That additional bit of information (the question) "bumps" the short-term memory out of your awareness.

Long-term memory

Although most unimportant short-term memories quickly decay, the brain stores the important ones— those that are emotionally compelling or personally meaningful. That stored information is long-term memory. It is the total of what you know: a compendium of data ranging from your name, address, and phone number and the names of friends and relatives to more complex information, such as the sounds and images of important events that happened decades ago. It also includes the routine information you use every day, like how to make coffee, operate your computer, and carry out all of the intricate behavioral sequences involved in performing your job or running your household.

Your long-term memory and short-term memory are not distinguished merely by how long the memories last. Another difference is the amount of information each memory system and its associated brain regions can handle. Although the brain can juggle only a relatively small number of short-term memories at a time, it can store an enormous number of long-term memories. Barring disease or injury, you can always learn and retain something new. Furthermore, long-term memories are less fragile than short-term memories, which means they're not lost when something interrupts your train of thought. Some types of previously learned long-term memories even tend to remain intact in the early stages of dementia, when patients have trouble learning new information (see "Dementia," page 17).

Maintaining a long-term memory often requires that you periodically "revisit" it. Some long-term memories that go unused or become irrelevant fade or become distorted over time. Have you ever read a book that you loved, but years later found yourself unable to recall much more than the title? That's probably because you hadn't thought of the plot and characters in a long time. On the other hand, some long-term memories are amazingly persistent, no matter how infrequently you use them. For example, many adults are surprised by their ability to remember minute details of their youth—an unjustified punishment they received, a fifth-grade science project, their first date. Interestingly, research demonstrates that although long-term memory is more durable than short-term memory, it is also changeable. For example, the way you remember your first romance can evolve over time in response to experiences and information you acquire years later.

Long-term memory can be divided into two categories: declarative memory and implicit memory. (We will discuss one form of implicit memory, called procedural memory).

Declarative memory

Also known as explicit memory, declarative memory is information that requires a conscious effort to recall. There are two types of declarative memory: semantic memory and episodic memory. Semantic memory is factual knowledge, such as the names of the continents, the color of your spouse's eyes, or what winter is. Much of the basic information you acquired during your school days falls into this category. In addition to being factual, semantic memory has another key characteristic: it is not bound to a specific point in time. You can't point to the exact moment when you learned that George Washington led the Revolutionary War, for example. And even if you can remember the specific day when you learned the multiplication tables or other facts in school, the timing isn't important to your knowledge of them.

By contrast, episodic memory contains the images and details of experiences you have had. Episodic memories are personal memories tied to specific times and places. The party you attended last weekend, the vacation you took last summer, and your children's birthday celebrations are all episodic memories. An episodic memory is more fragile than a semantic memory because it is more specific; it has a smaller network of associated connections in the brain. Throughout your lifetime, you've probably thought about George Washington being the first president of the United States a hundred or more times, in many different contexts—maybe during social studies class, then during a trip to see his historic house, then when you saw his head on a quarter, etc. Episodic memories, on the other hand, are probably brought up in fewer contexts and less often.

Although patients with Alzheimer's are frequently able to recall events from many years ago, they have profound difficulty acquiring new episodic memories. That's partly because a brain region called the hippocampus (see Figure 1), which plays a central role in memory encoding, is particularly vulnerable to degenerative disorders such as Alzheimer's disease. The frontal lobes and their connections also seem to be particularly vulnerable to age-related changes. The frontal lobes are essential in focusing attention and ignoring distractions, initiating strategies for the effective acquisition of new information, activating and retrieving stored memories, recollecting the source of information, and keeping track of the timing and order of specific events. The frontal lobes have been likened to the "file clerk" of the episodic memory system, the hippocampus and medial temporal lobes to the "recent memory file cabinet," and other cortical regions to the "remote memory file cabinet" (see Figure 2). Different anatomical nodes in the memory network are connected via "white matter" fiber bundles, which are commonly disrupted by age-related conditions including high blood pressure, diabetes, high cholesterol, and small vessel disease.

Flashbulb memory

Memory researchers use the term "flashbulb memory" to describe a vivid memory of an unexpected, emotionally charged public event. The assassination of President Kennedy and the destruction of the World Trade Center are examples of compelling public events that became ingrained in the memories of many who witnessed them, either directly or through television. Flashbulb memories tend to include numerous minute details associated with your experience of the event—where you were standing, what you were doing, who was around you, and so on. It is likely that the combination of profound meaningfulness and emotional impact surrounding the event serves to inscribe it intensively in long-term memory.

Experts used to assume that flashbulb memories remained more accurate over time than ordinary memories, but research has shown that they are vulnerable to the same biases and distortions as memories of less dramatic events.

This theory has been corroborated in studies of different groups of people in the aftermath of the Sept. 11, 2001, terrorist attack. In a 2009 study in *The Journal of Experimental Psychology*, researchers questioned more than 3,000 people from seven U.S. cities about their memories of the event one week, 11 months, and 35 months after the assault. Participants answered questions about where they were, what they were doing, and how they felt when they first heard the news, as well as specific facts about the attack, such as the number of planes involved (referred to as event memory). The researchers found that the rate of forgetting was about 20% or more the first year and between 5% and 10% thereafter—a rate that's similar to ordinary autobiographical memories.

Disruption of these pathways slows processing speed and undermines memory capacity.

Procedural memory

Procedural memory refers to memory for skills and routines. It is a form of implicit memory that allows your performance on a task to improve without conscious awareness of previous experiences. You draw on procedural memories automatically to perform actions like getting dressed or driving your car. How to ride a bicycle, write in cursive, operate a video recorder—each of these skills required effort and practice at one time, but once you mastered it, you were able to perform it without remembering how you learned it or the separate steps involved. When you take out your bike for a ride, you don't say to yourself, "Okay, first I straddle the seat, then I put my left foot on the left pedal, and then I push off the ground with my right foot…." You just get on and go. It's as though your body does the remembering for you.

In contrast to declarative memory, procedural memory is more resistant to aging and illness. Individuals with Alzheimer's can perform many routine tasks well into the disease process. This is because procedural memory is supported by different brain systems than declarative memory (the basal ganglia is one). These parts of the brain are relatively well-preserved in Alzheimer's disease. In contrast, patients with impairment of basal ganglia functioning (like in Parkinson's disease) often have impaired procedural memory, but relatively well-preserved episodic memory.

Similarly, studies of patients with amnesia who spend time each day practicing new activities, such as playing computer games, suggest that they can learn new skills. Although the amnesiac patients usually can't recall ever having played or even seen the computer games, their performance improves over time and with practice, indicating that they are capable of acquiring new procedural memories. ▼

How we remember

You just saw a new film, and stored it—along with other information and events that you encountered today—in your brain. But where, exactly, did it go? Is your brain's system for storing memories a "memory bank," a single repository of all the sights, sounds, and facts that have made a strong enough impression for you to remember them? Or is it a kind of library, with different memories categorized by something akin to the Dewey decimal system, and then stored in different "stacks" from which they can be retrieved?

Figure 2 Brain map

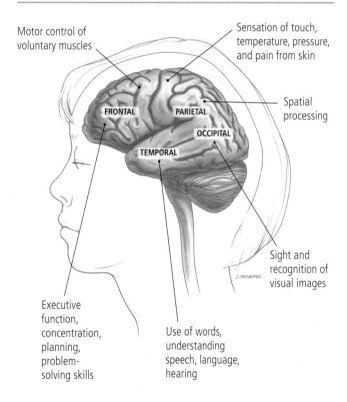

Motor control of voluntary muscles

Sensation of touch, temperature, pressure, and pain from skin

FRONTAL

PARIETAL

OCCIPITAL

TEMPORAL

Spatial processing

Sight and recognition of visual images

Executive function, concentration, planning, problem-solving skills

Use of words, understanding speech, language, hearing

Different parts of the brain specialize in different functions. Memories are stored in many parts of the brain, but some areas are more critical than others. To retrieve a memory, these areas of the brain must work in coordination with others. For example, the frontal lobe (important for planning and organization) works together with several brain regions in acquiring and retrieving memories.

As good as memories in the bank

One of the enduring myths about memories is that they are kept in one place in the brain, a memory bank. But over many decades of research, scientists realized that this assumption was wrong. In the 1980s, when functional brain-imaging technology—such as positron emission tomography (PET) scans—became available, scientists could more clearly observe people's brains at work for the first time (see "Watching the brain at work," page 44). They could obtain images of the brain as people performed a variety of tasks, including remembering things. Researchers confirmed that memories are not stored in a single location, but rather are widely distributed in networks throughout the brain, primarily in the cerebral cortex. The cerebral cortex consists of the outer covering of the two large hemispheres of the brain and is the most highly developed part of the human nervous system. The cortex contains about 20 billion neurons that collectively function to integrate sensory information, control voluntary movements, and mediate thinking processes.

Different areas of the brain process different kinds of information (see Figure 2). For example, auditory information, including speech and other sounds, is processed initially in the temporal lobes, while the registration of visual images occurs in the occipital lobe at the back of the brain. What these findings suggest is that a particular aspect of a memory will most likely be stored in a region of the cortex that specializes in processing similar information.

Therefore, the words of "The Star-Spangled Banner" would be stored in the language regions of the left temporal lobe, but the melody would be stored in different regions of the brain's auditory cortex. And each memory is connected to many related memories. For instance, if you associate "The Star-Spangled Banner" with the image of the American flag, that memory might be stored in your occipital lobe, which processes visual information. Your memories are thus intricately broken down and cross-referenced, making your brain less like the shelves of a library and more like the Internet. Calling up memories is like searching the Internet, with one or two words activating many hyperlinks.

But just how does the information that you encounter on a daily basis get filed away? Memory researchers have used a three-stage model to describe how the brain learns and remembers each bit of information:

1. acquisition
2. consolidation
3. retrieval.

Impairment in any one of these three stages can result in a failure of memory.

How smoothly the process goes—which is to say, how well you remember—depends on many things. Genetics plays a major role. Studies of human intelligence suggest that approximately 50% of mental ability is genetically determined. It may be that some people are simply better at remembering than others because of a genetic predisposition for an excellent memory. But factors within your control are also important. Overall physical health, emotional well-being, stress level, sleep quality, and diet exert a huge influence on how well you learn and remember.

Stage one: Acquisition

It's common sense: to remember anything, you must first learn it. When new information is learned or acquired, it first takes the form of temporary pathways of nerve cell activity in the brain, as one neuron communicates with the next. The location of these neuronal pathways depends on the nature of the information. For example, in most people, activities such as speaking and writing activate neurons in the left temporal lobe, which processes language, whereas studying a map activates neurons in the right parietal lobe, which processes spatial information (see Figure 2).

When you've just learned something new, the neuronal activity that represents the information you've just learned is temporary, and the new information is part of your short-term memory. Most of this information will quickly fade away. The memories that endure will be those that were encoded most completely in the first place—the information that you paid the closest attention to when you learned it. When you have trouble remembering a piece of information, it's often because you weren't paying close attention when you initially encountered it. One of the reasons older people have more trouble remembering things is that they are more easily distracted by background noises and other interruptions, which can interfere with initial learning. Memories that involve multiple senses as well as emotions are more likely to be retained.

Stage two: Consolidation

Let's say that you were paying close attention to the information you just heard and that it was effectively encoded in your brain. How does it become stored as a memory that you can recall in the future? For the information to become a long-term memory, its initial neuronal pathways must be strengthened. The strengthening process, typically referred to as consolidation, occurs over a period of time.

Consolidation of declarative memories

Several factors influence whether the hippocampus responds to the newly acquired information and gives the signal to store it as long-term memory. For example, you're more likely to retain new information if it relates to long-term memories you already have. It's easier to remember the names of the players on your local football team if you know something about football than if you don't follow the game at all. Another factor is the information's emotional impact (see Figure 3). You're far more likely to remember a disturbing photograph than a bland one. You can probably remember the images of the World Trade Center falling far more vividly than you can, say, a photo of a hotel where you attended a business conference. The part of the brain that reacts to emotionally powerful information is the amygdala, which is situated near the hippocampus. Some research using PET scans suggests information that activates the amygdala is most likely to be retained long-term.

Figure 3 Remember grandma's cookies?

An experience that stimulates many parts of the brain is more likely to be remembered, particularly if it has an emotional component.

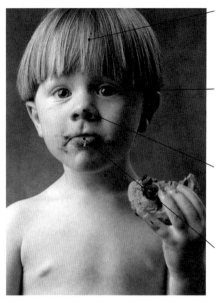

EMOTION: Feelings of pleasure are processed by the amygdala, a structure deep in the brain.

SIGHT: The eye relays the image of chocolate chip cookies to the primary visual cortex in the occipital lobe.

SMELL: Sensors in the nose pick up the sweet scent and convey it to the olfactory region of the cortex.

TASTE: Sensory receptors on the tongue deliver the flavor of chocolate to the brain's gustatory area.

Consolidation of procedural memories

In contrast to declarative memory, the consolidation of procedural memories is not dependent on the hippocampus. Even people with amnesia, who have damage to the hippocampus, can form new procedural memories—that is to say, they can learn new skills through practice. Procedural memories, such as how to play a musical instrument, also tend to remain intact with aging. They even persist during the early stages of Alzheimer's disease, which damages the hippocampus. However, acquiring new procedural memories becomes more difficult with age because we process information more slowly.

Procedural memory is stored throughout the brain in regions that are important for coordinating movement or sequential processing, such as the frontal lobes, the cerebellum, and the basal ganglia. Studies also show that sleep is vital for consolidating procedural memory. In an experiment at Harvard University, students who learned a computer game were better able to remember it and play it the next day if they'd had more than six hours of sleep than if they'd had less. Even two days to a week later, students who were consistently well-rested outperformed those who didn't sleep as well.

Stage three: Retrieval

Retrieval is the act of recalling something. A memory is stored in the brain as a unique pattern of nerve cell activation. When you're not thinking about the memory, its neuronal pattern is inactive. To retrieve the information, your brain must reactivate the pattern. Similar memories have partially overlapping patterns of neuronal activation. Sometimes when you try to retrieve one bit of information, a similar memory comes to mind and blocks out the information you want. For example, you may be trying to recall the name of Tom Hanks' first movie, but instead you keep thinking of the name of his most recent film.

Researchers have determined that it takes less than a second to reactivate a neuronal pathway holding simple, familiar information. They've found, for example, that when a young person sees a photograph and is asked whether it's familiar, it takes about a fifth of a second for the image to reach the visual system in the brain, a fifth of a second for the person to decide whether it's familiar, and another fifth of a second for the person to generate a motor response.

If it always took just a fraction of a second to remember something, you wouldn't worry about your memory. But, of course, it often takes considerably longer. Even if your memory is perfect, it can take several seconds or more to recall complicated information. How long the process takes depends on how familiar you are with the information you're looking for. If someone asks you to name the third president of the United States, for example, and you're an American history teacher, you may be able to recall in an instant that the answer is Thomas Jefferson. Otherwise, your brain will activate neuronal pathways that encode information related to the chronology of the presidents—the year when the United States was founded and the names of any early presidents that come to mind, for instance. In the process, you may feel that the answer is "on the tip of your tongue." If the neuronal pathway in your brain leading to the answer is still intact, you'll eventually retrieve it. ◆

Forgetting: What's normal?

It's normal to forget some things, and it's normal to become somewhat more forgetful as you age, but it's not normal to forget too much. The question is, how much is too much? Regardless of age, some people's memories are better than others—just as some people are better at math or athletics. How can you tell whether your memory lapses are within the scope of normal aging or are a symptom of something more serious?

Neuroscientists and physicians have not fully answered that question, but they have identified some key differences between normal memory lapses and those that occur with more serious cognitive deficits, such as dementia, a progressive deterioration of memory and other aspects of cognitive function.

Seven types of normal memory problems

Regardless of age, healthy people can experience memory loss or memory distortion. Daniel Schacter, a professor of psychology at Harvard University, describes seven common "sins" of memory, discussed below. Some of these memory flaws become more pronounced with age, but—unless they are extreme and persistent—they are not considered indicators of Alzheimer's or other memory-impairing illnesses.

Transience

This is the tendency to forget facts or events over time. You are most likely to forget information soon after you learn it. However, memory has a use-it-or-lose-it quality: memories that are called up and used frequently are least likely to be forgotten. Although transience might seem like a sign of memory weakness, brain scientists regard it as beneficial because it clears the brain of unused memories, making way for newer, more useful ones. In this sense, transience is akin to cleaning the junk out of your closets or clearing the temporary files from your computer's hard drive.

Although everyone experiences transience of memory, it is extreme and debilitating in people with particular kinds of brain damage. For instance, people with amnesia from damage to the hippocampus and related structures have normal short-term memory, but they are unable to form new long-term memories (see "Amnesia: Memory loss caused by injury or trauma," page 15). They forget information soon after they learn it.

Absentmindedness

This type of forgetting occurs when you don't pay close enough attention. You forget where you just put your pen because you didn't focus on where you put it in the first place. You were thinking of something else (or, perhaps, nothing in particular), so your brain didn't encode the information securely. Absentmindedness also involves forgetting to do something at a prescribed time, like taking your medicine or keeping an appointment.

One way to avoid this problem is to identify things that can serve as cues to remind you to do something. For example, if the doctor tells you to take your medicine at bedtime, you might use another regular bedtime activity as a reminder cue for medicine-taking. In this situation, you could link it to rinsing after toothbrushing, and use the same water glass to sip water to take your pills. Similarly, if you need to take your vitamins at breakfast, you could make a habit of putting the bottle beside your coffee cup at your place at the table so it provides a cue when you sit down to eat.

Blocking

Someone asks you a question and the answer is right on the tip of your tongue—you know that you know it, but you just can't think of it. This tip-of-the-tongue experience is perhaps the most familiar example of blocking, the temporary inability to retrieve a memory.

Blocking doesn't occur because you weren't paying attention or because the memory you're looking for has faded from your brain. On the contrary, blocking occurs when a memory is properly stored in your brain, but something is keeping you from finding it.

In many cases, the memory block is a memory similar to the one you're looking for, and you retrieve the wrong one. This competing memory is so intrusive that you can't think of the memory you want. A common example is calling your older son by your younger son's name, or vice versa. Scientists call blocking memories "ugly sisters" because they're domineering, like the stepsisters in Cinderella. Scientists have used ugly sisters experimentally to block memories. In one such experiment, people were asked to pick out the definitions of uncommon words from a selection of possible definitions. When definitions that were similar in sound or in meaning were given along with the accurate definition, more people had memory blocks than when unrelated ones were given.

Brain-imaging studies suggest how blocking might work in the brain. When a person is retrieving a memory, some regions of the brain become more active and others become less active. Some of the increased activation reflects inhibition of other regions. When the right regions are activated, this inhibition can work in your favor by keeping your brain from calling up irrelevant information. But when you call up an ugly sister by mistake, the brain regions that encode it may suppress the regions needed to retrieve the memory you really want.

Scientists think that memory blocks become more common with age and that they account for the trouble older people have remembering other people's names. But it remains unclear whether tip-of-the-tongue experiences are more common than other age-related memory problems. Increases in blocking have been linked to less efficient executive control mechanisms that help keep competing memories or words from interfering with the selection of the appropriate response. In any case, there's encouraging news about blocking. Research shows that people are able to retrieve about half of the blocked memories within just a minute.

Misattribution

Consider the following scenario: you're asked who "John Smith" is, and you remember quite clearly not only who he is, but also what he's done lately that's been in the news. Then you're asked where you learned these details. You think for a moment and reply that it was on the evening TV news. However, there was no report about John Smith on TV. Instead, you got your information from the friend you had lunch with yesterday.

Right memory, wrong source—that's one example of misattribution. Misattribution occurs when you remember something accurately in part, but misattribute some detail, like the time, place, or person involved. Another kind of misattribution occurs when you believe a thought you had was totally original when, in fact, it came from something you had previously read or heard but had forgotten about. This sort of misattribution explains cases of unintentional plagiarism, in which a writer passes off some information as original when he or she actually read it somewhere before.

Misattribution happens to everyone. Usually it's harmless, but it can have profound consequences, particularly in the criminal justice system. In some cases, misattribution on the part of eyewitnesses is responsible for the arrest and conviction of individuals for crimes they didn't commit.

As with several other kinds of memory lapses, misattribution becomes more common with age. Age matters in at least two ways. First, as you age, you absorb fewer details when acquiring information because you have somewhat more trouble concentrating and processing information rapidly. Second, as you grow older, your memories grow older as well. And old memories are especially prone to misattribution.

Suggestibility

Imagine that you saw someone fleeing from a car as its antitheft alarm was blaring. You didn't get a good look at the thief, but another person on the street insisted that it was a man wearing a green plaid jacket. Later, when the police show you photos of possible suspects, you're confused until you see a man dressed in green plaid. Then you point to him.

Suggestibility is the vulnerability of your memory to the power of suggestion—information that you learn about an occurrence after the fact. Although little is known about exactly how suggestibility works in the brain, the suggestion fools your mind into thinking it's a real memory. Suggestibility can be the culprit in recollections that adults have of incidents from their childhood that never really happened.

Bias

One of the enduring myths about memory is that it works like a camera, recording what you perceive and experience with complete, objective accuracy. But even the sharpest memory isn't a flawless snapshot of reality. In your memory, your perceptions are filtered by your personal biases—experiences, beliefs, prior knowledge, and even your mood at the moment. Your biases affect your perceptions and experiences when they're being encoded in your brain. And when you retrieve a memory, your mood and other biases at that moment can influence what information you actually recall.

Bias can affect all sorts of memories, but among the most interesting examples are people's recollections of their romantic relationships. In one study, couples who were dating were asked to evaluate themselves, their partners, and their relationships—initially and then two months later. During the second session, participants were asked to recall what they had said initially. The people whose feelings for their partners and their relationships had become more negative over time recalled their initial evaluations as more negative than they really were. On the other hand, people whose feelings for their partners and their relationships had become more loving recalled their initial evaluations as more positive than they really were.

Although everyone's attitudes and preconceived notions bias their memories, one group of people in which this concept plays a bitter role is people prone to depression. These people tend to have what's called negative memory bias: they remember negative information better than positive information.

Negative memory bias is an important risk factor for depression, which makes sense—constantly remembering the sad things that happened to you more than the happy things is likely to help sustain a depressed mood.

Researchers are looking into which parts of the brain are involved in negative memory bias. Some theories suggest a problem with the way the amygdala and hippocampus interact. Another study implies that a small-sized hippocampus relative to the size of the amygdala might be related to negative memory bias. These results make sense given that the hippocampus is a part of the brain that processes factual memories, whereas the amygdala processes emotional memories. One area of research that still needs to be probed is whether memory bias of any kind becomes more common with age.

Persistence

Most people worry about forgetting things. But in some cases people are tormented by memories they wish they could forget, but can't. The persistence of memories of traumatic events, negative feelings, and ongoing fears is another form of memory problem. Some of these memories accurately reflect horrifying events, while others may be negative distortions of reality.

Two groups of people are particularly prone to having persistent, disturbing memories. One group is individuals with depression. Research has shown that depressed people are given to ruminating over unpleasant events in their lives or mistakes that they believe they have made. Dwelling on such negatives also fuels a vicious cycle of increasing depression. The other group with persistent, unwanted memories includes people with post-traumatic stress disorder (PTSD). PTSD can result from many different forms of traumatic exposure—for example, sexual abuse or wartime experiences. Flashbacks, which are persistent, intrusive memories of the traumatic event, are a core feature of PTSD. ◗

How memory changes with age

For many people, memory loss becomes noticeable after about age 50. However, changes in aspects of memory function are detectable with neuropsychological testing as early as the 20s and 30s. This is similar to other physical traits, such as athletic performance, which also peaks in early adulthood. But one of the myths surrounding the term "age-related memory loss" is that all memories slip with the passing years. In fact, while some information may become harder to recall—and new memories may be harder to lay down in the brain—other memories will remain as accessible as ever.

In particular, there is truth in the old saying that "you never forget how to ride a bicycle." Procedural memory—by which you remember processes and skills such as how to ride a bicycle, serve a tennis ball, or accomplish routine tasks—does not fade with age. In fact, it's so resilient that it remains intact even in people with early- to mid-stage Alzheimer's.

Visual memories, on the other hand, may be less resilient. While some research shows that older people's recall of images such as faces is comparable to that of young people's, other studies suggest a significant decline in older people's ability to remember new images. In one, adults of different ages were asked to look at 18 detailed colored pictures; three days later, they were shown several of these pictures as well as others, and asked which ones they'd seen before. Between 60% and 70% of older participants' memories were inaccurate, compared with just 25% to 35% of younger people's memories.

Why memory fades

Brain regions involved with memory processing, such as the hippocampus and especially the frontal lobes, undergo age-related structural and neurochemical changes. These changes can undermine the encoding, consolidation, and retrieval of new information.

Different kinds of memory can decline with age, including

- the episodic form of declarative memory (e.g., which stock you sold last year from your retirement account)
- the semantic form of declarative memory (e.g., facts, such as the exact year World War I started)
- spatial memory (e.g., the directions to a new location).

It's not just that you learn this sort of information more slowly; you may have more trouble recalling it because you hadn't fully learned it in the first place.

Some of what scientists know about age-related memory loss comes from studies of animals. In one such study, older mice took longer to learn to escape from a maze than younger mice. These results are consistent with what scientists observe in people—and what people notice about themselves as they age. If you and your child or grandchild learn a new computer game together, chances are that the next day the child will remember more of the details of how to play the game than you do.

Willpower and effort can overcome some age-related difficulties with learning. Researchers now know that in many instances, if you make the effort to learn something well, you will be rewarded—you'll be able to recall it as well as a younger person can (see "Behavioral strategies," page 36).

When brain cells die

For years, the scientific view of an adult's brain was anything but encouraging. Experts believed that your brain produced new brain cells only early in life and that once you reached adulthood, the growth of new neurons ceased and existing neurons began to die off. You may have heard the oft-repeated "fact" that you lose 10,000 brain cells a day. The idea was that your brain was shrinking, and that could mean only one thing: as you lost neurons, you also lost some of your capacity to learn, think, and remember.

Researchers now know that this brain cell degradation is less pronounced than previously thought. Still, the effects may be significant: in many older people, the loss of neurons affects the activity of neurotransmitters, chemicals that provide the means for communication among cells in the brain and nervous system. The aging brain seems to lose neurons in structures deep within the brain that produce neurotransmitters, such as dopamine, acetylcholine, and serotonin, all of which are important for learning and memory (see Figure 4).

Animal research suggests that the age-related decline in the ability to learn new information may, in part, reflect a decline in the level of dopamine in the brain's frontal cortex. For example, young rabbits learn new tasks better than older rabbits, and older rabbits have half the dopamine activity in several key brain regions. Similar results have been found in monkeys. When dopamine-rich areas of monkeys' brains are damaged, the animals exhibit a significant impairment in attention and vigilance. Finally, when dopamine-producing neurons are transplanted into the brains of aging rats, their cognitive function improves. In a small human experiment, researchers concluded that dopamine enhances the strength of connections between neurons related to learning, and decreases the "excitability" of the connections between other types of neurons. This function could be one way dopamine improves memory and learning.

Perhaps of greater importance, some receptors may cease to function normally. Receptors are the points on neurons where neurotransmitters attach themselves. These receptors play a major role in helping the neurotransmitters involved in learning and memory move from one neuron to another. The effects of these age-related changes are especially noticeable in regions of the brain involved in attention and memory, such as the frontal lobes. The result is that as you age, it takes longer to absorb new information as well as to form new memories.

In addition, the loss of neurons and receptors may make it harder to concentrate. The ability to perform tasks involving attention and executive function (see "Testing executive function," page 43) declines with age. Thus, when people of all ages encounter new information, they may all take in the big picture, but those who are older may not absorb as much detail. For instance, after listening to a presentation, a 25-year-old and a 75-year-old may both remember the overall subject and basic ideas, but the 25-year-old may be able to recall more of the specifics.

These changes may sound disturbing, but neuroscientists actually consider them relatively minor as long as they're strictly a sign of aging and

Figure 4 A wide web of memories

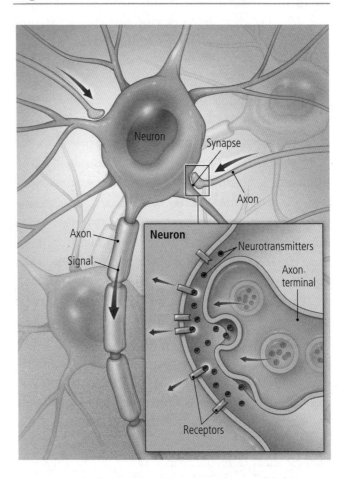

A vast network of interconnecting neurons (brain cells) delivers and permanently stores messages along pathways in the brain, primarily in the cerebral cortex, the large, domed outer layer of the brain. Scientists now know that memories are not stored in a single area but in a network of different areas of the brain. Brain cells communicate from one cell to the next across spaces called synapses, by way of chemical substances. These neurotransmitters activate the receptors on the neighboring cell's body or on long tentacle-like dendrites.

not of an illness such as Alzheimer's disease. In other words, age-related changes in the brain may slow down your learning and your recall and may make it harder for you to apply strategies for learning. But ultimately, they don't impair your ability to function effectively. For example, they have no effect on your ability to make sense of what you know or to form reasonable arguments and judgments. Your wisdom gained from experience remains unscathed. Brain scientists have found that people can compensate for the slowdown in information processing and diminished ability to concentrate if they work harder at paying attention when they encounter something new and consolidate the new information by repeating it in their minds and using it—for example, by talking about it with friends (see "Memory-enhancing techniques," page 38).

Growing new brain cells

Another surprise in our concept of brain aging concerns the growth of new neurons, a process known as neurogenesis. In the early 1970s, researchers found that adult rats and guinea pigs did in fact grow new neurons. The same proved true for cats, chickadees, tree shrews, and marmoset monkeys. But most scientists clung to the assumption that adult humans were different from these animals until 1998, when they found compelling evidence to the contrary.

The evidence came from a study of five people who had died of cancer. Before their deaths, their brains had been injected with a chemical that helped doctors count the number of new cells. The intent was to count the number of new cancer cells, but the chemical also revealed new healthy cells. Sure enough, all five patients had recently sprouted new healthy neurons, and these neurons were in the hippocampus. This finding was nothing short of revolutionary. It transformed the way neuroscientists think about the aging brain and memory.

But many questions remain unanswered about neuron growth in the human brain. Although researchers now know that the brain normally creates thousands of neurons each day, most of these cells die in the first weeks of their existence. And the mechanisms behind the birth and death of these cells are still largely a mystery. However, research on rodents may point to answers for some of these questions. A 2006 study in *The Journal of Neuroscience* hinted that when rodents were taught tasks that engaged several areas in the brain, more new hippocampal cells survived. Plus, there was a direct relationship between how much the animals learned and the number of surviving cells. Even cells that were born before the animals began the learning exercises had a better chance of survival. In another study in *The Journal of Neuroscience* in 2007, researchers demonstrated that when brain-injured mice were treated with grafted stem cells, they recovered their memory function to the point where it equaled that of healthy mice. Finding ways to use stem cells to treat neurodegenerative diseases, such as Parkinson's disease, remains a hot topic for research, but translating the biology of stem cells into a therapy for patients is likely many years away. In a review paper on the subject of stem cell therapy and neurodegenerative diseases published in 2011 in the *Annals of Neurology*, the authors wrote that getting the therapy "from bench to bedside may take well over a decade."

Changes in brain structure

Brain tissue can be divided into two categories—white matter and gray matter. The gray matter contains the neurons, while the white matter contains the insulated "wires" (axons) that run between the neurons, connecting them to each other. Both "colors" are important. Many studies have shown that loss of or damage to white matter in people who are aging normally (meaning those without Alzheimer's disease or mild cognitive impairment) is associated with a decline in executive function, working memory, and speed of processing. Cerebrovascular disease (damage to the blood vessels leading to the brain that reduces blood flow to the brain and can cause stroke) may be at the root of these changes, but this is a matter of debate. Although uncertainties remain, it seems prudent to reduce cardiac risk factors (see "Cardiovascular disease and its risk factors," page 20).

Other possible biological causes for a decline in mental capacity as a person ages are reduced connections between brain cells, diminished gray matter volume, and less availability of neurotransmitters like dopamine. ▼

Memory impairment: Normal aging or brain disease?

Normal cognitive aging leads to predictable changes in thinking and memory that are associated with getting older. It differs from pathological aging caused by diseases that damage the brain, such as Alzheimer's or cerebrovascular disease. The normal aging process includes "wear and tear" damage from oxidative stress, reduced capacity to detoxify molecules or proteins that are harmful to brain cells, and declines in the energy-generating components of cells (mitochondria) that allow them to function optimally. Neurodegenerative diseases like Alzheimer's lead to a cascade of events that accelerate cellular dysfunction and death and are often associated with the accumulation of toxic proteins.

Although mild age-related memory loss is considered normal, more severe memory impairment is not (see Table 1). When neurons are damaged or cannot function effectively, memory loss and a slowdown in information processing—known collectively as cognitive decline—can occur. The following are some examples of conditions that prevent neurons from functioning normally, causing a variety of mental impairments, including memory loss.

Mild cognitive impairment

People with mild cognitive impairment (MCI) have either memory loss, decline of other mental functions, or both, which are more persistent and severe than what is considered normal for their age, but are less severe than what is found in people with dementia. MCI has two major subtypes: amnestic (when memory is impaired) and nonamnestic (when other types of cognitive functioning, such as use of language, navigation, or attention, are affected). If a person has impairments in both categories, he or she would fall into a category known as MCI, multi-domain.

In addition to being more severe than normal age-related memory loss, MCI is also different in terms

Amnesia: Memory loss caused by injury or trauma

Amnesia is the inability to form new memories or, in some cases, to remember existing ones. Amnesia occurs when key structures of the brain—such as the hippocampus, which is essential for encoding memories—don't function properly. Some types of stroke, concussive injury, chronic alcoholism, disruption of oxygen supply, or certain kinds of infections such as viral encephalitis can cause amnesia. It is also a common side effect of electroconvulsive therapy used to treat major depression, although the effect is typically temporary.

People with amnesia don't forget everything, and they retain their general level of intelligence. They have a normal attention span and can form short-term memories lasting perhaps a few minutes. Their procedural memory—which covers well-established skills such as driving a car or brushing their teeth—remains intact, because retention of these skills doesn't depend on the hippocampus and surrounding brain structures. The breakdown occurs with acquiring new long-term declarative memories, which often depend on the hippocampus. People with anterograde amnesia are unable to form new long-term memories after an injury or the onset of illness. People with retrograde amnesia have difficulty retrieving previously learned information, memories that had been acquired before the onset of the condition that caused the amnesia.

The duration of amnesia depends on the cause. If the disruption of brain function is temporary (as in a blow to the head that causes a minor concussion), most of the lost memory will be restored, although memories formed just before and soon after the injury occurred may be lost forever.

There is also a rare condition called transient global amnesia (TGA). TGA refers to a brief period of time (usually hours) during which a person is able to engage in normal behavior but after which she or he does not remember the events that occurred during that period. TGA is not related to later development of a more serious memory disorder such as Alzheimer's disease, although the actual cause of the condition is unknown. Emotionally or physically stressful events such as intense physical activity, sudden immersion in hot or cold water, sexual intercourse, or medical procedures can trigger an episode. TGA tends to be more frequent in people who get migraines. Certain drugs and medications can also produce TGA-like episodes.

of the kind of information a person forgets. With normal memory loss, people tend to forget things that aren't terribly important to them—the name of a casual acquaintance, for example, or to go to a dental cleaning. With MCI, a person may not be able to learn and retain important new information, such as the record of a favorite sports team, the outcome of important political events, or the plans of close friends or family members.

When taking memory tests, people with the amnestic type of MCI have more trouble remembering the details of pictures they've seen or paragraphs they've read just a few minutes earlier. Their memory difficulty is comparable to that of someone with very mild Alzheimer's disease. But on tests that measure other mental functions, such as their ability to keep the details of routine activities straight, people with this type of MCI perform as well as healthy people and much better than people with Alzheimer's. The critical difference between someone with MCI and someone with dementia is that in the person with MCI, the cognitive impairment does not yet substantially interfere with day-to-day functioning.

The prevalence of MCI isn't well defined, mostly because studies have used different definitions of the condition. One meta-analysis came to the conclusion that somewhere between 5% and 25% of seniors ages 65 and older had MCI. This was based on three studies done on older adults living in the community. Another analysis of participants in a cardiovascular health study estimated that 19% of those ages 65 to 74, and 29% of those older than 85, had MCI.

To diagnose MCI, the doctor obtains a thorough medical history and conducts neuropsychological or cognitive testing (see "When to see a doctor," page 42). The determination of whether a person's social and occupational functioning remains intact—the crucial factor differentiating MCI from dementia—depends on a clinician's judgment based on input from the patient and loved ones.

The symptoms of amnestic MCI include

- a subjective sense of failing memory, preferably backed up by another person such as a family member (for example, the person reports being very forgetful, or that his or her memory is much worse than in the past)
- memory impairment (for age and education) as determined by testing

Table 1 Normal aging or dementia?

Physicians often use information like that summarized in this table to help differentiate between normal aging and dementia.

NORMAL AGING	DEMENTIA
The person remains independent in daily activities.	The person is critically dependent on others for key daily living activities.
The person complains of memory loss but can provide considerable detail regarding incidents of forgetfulness.	The person complains of memory problems only if specifically asked and cannot recall instances when memory loss was noticeable.
The individual is more concerned about perceived forgetfulness than close family members are.	Close family members are much more concerned than the individual is about incidents of memory loss.
Recent memory for important events, affairs, and conversations is not impaired.	Recent memory for events and ability to converse are both noticeably impaired.
The person has occasional difficulty finding words.	The person makes frequent word-finding pauses and substitutions.
The person does not get lost in familiar territory, but may have to pause momentarily to remember the way.	The person gets lost in familiar territory while walking or driving and may take hours to return home.
The individual operates common appliances even if she or he is unwilling to learn how to operate new devices.	The person cannot operate common appliances and is unable to learn to operate even simple new appliances.
There is no decline in interpersonal social skills.	The person may lose interest in social activities or exhibits socially inappropriate behaviors.
Performance on mental status examinations is normal relative to the individual's age, education, and culture.	Performance on mental status examinations is below normal in ways not accounted for by educational or cultural factors.

Source: Adapted from Diagnosis, Management and Treatment of Dementia: A Practical Guide for Primary Care Physicians (American Medical Association).

- essentially normal general cognitive function
- no difficulties carrying out activities of daily living
- no dementia.

Getting diagnosed with MCI can be frightening, especially because it is associated with a significant increase in the risk of developing dementia, particularly Alzheimer's disease. About 1% to 2% of the general population over age 65 develops dementia every year, but among those with MCI, it's 10% to 15%. Of the MCI patients who go on to develop some form of dementia, a large portion end up with Alzheimer's disease. MCI patients who carry the ApoE E4 allele (see "Genetic links to memory loss," page 19) face a higher risk for developing Alzheimer's dementia, as do those who have specific abnormalities on brain scans (e.g., atrophy of the hippocampus on MRI, or decreased metabolic activity in the temporal and parietal cortex on functional imaging studies) or abnormal levels of certain proteins in their spinal fluid.

Dementia

Dementia isn't a disease, per se. Instead, it's a descriptive term for a host of symptoms caused by a number of disorders that affect the brain. Although memory loss is a common symptom, memory loss by itself does not signify dementia. With dementia, people lose their cognitive abilities to the extent that they are unable to carry out normal activities and relationships. They may also experience personality and behavior changes such as agitation and delusions. Based on estimates from the Aging, Demographics, and Memory Study (ADAMS), about 14% of Americans 71 and older have some type of dementia. According to the Alzheimer's Association, other studies use a broader definition of dementia, and therefore the ADAMS figure might underrepresent the problem. Following are short summaries of the different forms.

■ **Alzheimer's disease.** Alzheimer's disease is far and away the leading cause of dementia, accounting for 60% to 80% of all dementia cases in elderly people. Although it is extremely rare before age 60, Alzheimer's, like dementia in general, becomes much more com-

mon with age. The disease involves a substantial loss of neurons along with the appearance of abnormal structures in the brain called plaques and tangles, particularly in regions of the brain associated with memory. Eventually, these abnormalities and the loss of neurons extend into other areas of the cortex.

The vast majority of people who develop Alzheimer's disease with symptoms starting after age 65 have no family history of early-onset Alzheimer's disease (meaning disease that starts before age 60). But in a small number of cases where symptoms begin earlier in life, the disease has a strong familial basis (see "Genetic links to memory loss," page 19).

■ **Vascular dementia.** Another common cause of dementia, vascular dementia refers to cognitive impairment that stems from damage to blood vessels

Figure 5 What happens during an ischemic stroke

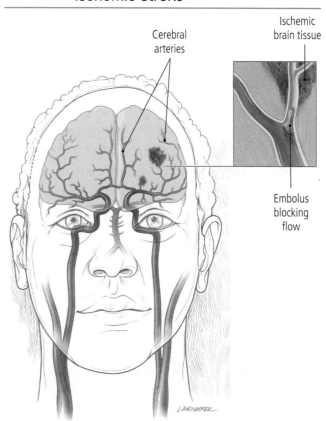

Cerebral arteries

Ischemic brain tissue

Embolus blocking flow

Ischemia refers to an insufficient supply of blood to an organ. Most strokes—about 87%—are so-called ischemic strokes, which are caused by blockage to an artery in the brain. Many of these ischemic strokes are caused by emboli, blood clots that travel to the brain after forming elsewhere, typically in the heart or aorta.

▶ Recognizing dementia

Although people in the earliest stages of dementia often sense that something is wrong, the illness eventually deprives them of the insight necessary to understand their problems. So it's usually up to a family member or friend to recognize the symptoms. If you suspect that someone you know has dementia, arrange for a medical evaluation. Many forms of dementia are not reversible, but early detection provides an opportunity to minimize other medical conditions that may bring out severe dementia symptoms earlier than they might otherwise show themselves. It also allows family members more time to come to terms with the illness and to plan for long-term care. There are several medications approved for the treatment of dementia that can bring about moderate, temporary improvement in memory and other elements of cognitive function (see "Medications for memory impairment," page 46). Symptoms commonly associated with dementia, such as depression, also can be addressed.

that feed the brain (see Figure 5). These vessels may become narrowed or blocked. Many factors, including high blood pressure and high cholesterol, may contribute to this damage (see "Cardiovascular disease and its risk factors," page 20).

Brain cells, like tissues elsewhere in the body, need a constant supply of oxygen to live; they get this oxygen from the blood. When blood flow is interrupted during a stroke, some brain cells die. Dementia symptoms can develop after a stroke. A 2010 article in the journal *Stroke* that reviewed data from 16 different studies concluded that for people 65 and older, having a stroke doubles the risk of developing dementia. Even "silent" strokes, or transient ischemic attacks (TIAs)—those that cause few or no obvious persisting motor or sensory symptoms but damage brain tissue—can lead to dementia. According to a large study published in *The New England Journal of Medicine* in 2003, people who had TIAs were more than twice as likely to develop dementia within three and a half years, on average, compared with people who had not had strokes. Since then, other, smaller studies have supported the fact that people who have suffered TIAs have a higher risk of dementia. People who experience this type of stroke also exhibit a sharper decline in memory test performance as well as in overall intellectual functioning. This effect might be explained by the fact that TIAs often occur in the brain's white matter, which contains the "wiring" that allows communication between brain regions.

■ **Mixed dementia.** Dementia is very often the outcome of more than one underlying disease process. The most common mixed dementia involves a combination of Alzheimer's disease and vascular dementia. In fact, it has been estimated that over 40% of patients with Alzheimer's disease also have cerebrovascular disease. But other mixed dementias, such as a combination of Alzheimer's disease and Lewy body dementia (see below), are also seen.

■ **Other types of dementia.** Several other brain disorders may also lead to dementia:

• *Dementia with Lewy bodies.* This progressive form of dementia stems from a buildup of abnormal proteins called Lewy bodies in brain cells that control cognitive functions and movement. According to the Lewy Body Dementia Association, this type of dementia affects 1.3 million Americans. The cognitive symptoms include problems with executive function, attention, processing speed, visuospatial abilities, and memory. People with this form of dementia often experience varying levels of alertness, sleep disturbances, visual hallucinations, and mild motor symptoms of Parkinson's disease.

• *Parkinson's disease dementia (PDD).* For dementia to be termed Parkinson's disease dementia, the person must have had Parkinson's disease for one year or more before the dementia came on. In PDD, like in Lewy body dementia, symptoms include impaired attention, impaired visuospatial function, problems retrieving information, and difficulties with executive function. Dementia is very common in people with Parkinson's disease, though just how common is hard to say. Studies suggest that close to one-third of patients with Parkinson's disease suffer from some form of dementia, and close to a third of Parkinson's disease patients without dementia meet criteria for mild cognitive impairment. Another thing that is unclear about PDD is whether it is a form of Lewy body dementia or a separate type of dementia. One thing is clear: cognitive symptoms often develop in the later stages of Parkinson's disease.

• *Frontotemporal dementia (FTD).* This group of diseases causes neurons in the frontal and temporal lobes of the brain to die. The symptoms depend on the part of the brain affected, but the most common signs include extreme changes in behavior and personality, such as inappropriate behavior, a lack of inhibition, euphoria, or—in contrast—apathy. Other forms may affect language or movement. It is sometimes misdiagnosed as a psychiatric disorder or Alzheimer's disease, but tends to occur at a younger age than is typically seen with Alzheimer's, usually from the mid-50s to the mid-60s. Of those with FTD, 20% to 40% have a family history of dementia, suggesting the illness often has a genetic component.

Head trauma

A blow to the head that is strong enough to cause a concussion—a brief alteration of consciousness—can also impair memory. The blow can damage brain cells, or it can stretch or tear the axons, the fine filament "tails" of the neurons that compose the white matter of the brain and spinal cord. Most people who suffer mild concussions recover their memories and other mental functions completely within a few hours or days.

More severe head trauma, such as an injury sustained in a high-speed collision, frequently destroys brain tissue and injures nerve fibers throughout the brain. This type of damage is permanent. People who sustain multiple injuries from concussion—prizefighters, for example—are prone to later development of dementia and other brain disorders. There's also evidence that repeated concussions raise the risk of traumatic encephalopathy, a serious and progressive condition. It starts with memory loss, confusion, dizziness, and headaches. Serious cases may progress to include symptoms of Parkinson's disease and dementia.

There is a growing awareness of reduced cognitive function caused by sports activities that involve impacts to the head that can result in repetitive concussions. These include football, soccer, lacrosse, and ice hockey. Many professional organizations, universities, and secondary schools in the United States have put into place concussion prevention and management guidelines. Prevention is clearly the best medicine here, but if you or someone you love does get a concussion, it's important to follow your doctor's orders when it comes to rest and rehabilitation. Studies show that quiet time is important for brain recovery post-concussion.

Other neurological disorders

Among the many illnesses that interfere with brain activities—including memory—are multiple sclerosis, epilepsy, brain tumors, Lyme disease that affects the brain, Huntington's disease, Creutzfeldt-Jakob disease, and late-stage AIDS. ▼

Genetic links to memory loss

Although this report emphasizes the many ways you can protect and enhance your memory and thinking, some things are beyond your control—including the genes you inherit from your parents. Dozens of studies involving more than 10,000 pairs of twins have shown that genetic differences account for about half of the variation in people's mental abilities. Your genetic makeup also affects the degree to which you experience age-related memory loss and your risk for conditions that can impair memory, such as high blood pressure and Alzheimer's disease. If your parents or siblings have memory loss, you are at higher risk than others who do not have this problem in their families.

There are two categories of genes that play a role in whether you develop Alzheimer's (or any inheritable disease, for that matter): risk genes and deterministic genes. Risk genes, as the name implies, increase your risk or chance of getting a disease. In Alzheimer's, the most influential risk gene is called apolipoprotein E4 (APO E4). This one gene might be a factor in 20% to 25% of Alzheimer's cases. Everyone inherits some version of the apolipoprotein E gene from each parent. Someone who inherits the E4 type from one parent has a higher risk of Alzheimer's; someone who inherits that gene from both parents has an even greater risk. But still, inheriting the E4 gene from both parents doesn't guarantee that a person will get Alzheimer's.

Genes in the second category—deterministic genes—don't just increase one's risk for a disease, they actually cause it. When this is the case in Alzheimer's disease, it's called autosomal dominant Alzheimer's disease (ADAD) or familial Alzheimer's disease. The genes responsible are variations in the genes that code three proteins: amyloid precursor protein (APP), presenilin-1 (PS-1), and presenilin-2 (PS-2). This type of Alzheimer's is responsible for the early-onset variety, which affects people before age 60 and often in their 30s or 40s. Since these genes always cause Alzheimer's, families that pass them from one generation to the next suffer generation after generation of early-onset disease. Fortunately, these genes are rare, so familial Alzheimer's only accounts for less than 5% of Alzheimer's cases.

Health and lifestyle factors linked to memory problems

Many people assume that memory loss is exclusively caused by either aging or Alzheimer's disease. In truth, a wide range of risk factors—including medical disorders, medications, and even lifestyle factors—can contribute to memory loss. Several common health problems, such as high blood pressure, become more common with age and, together with age-related changes in the brain, help explain why you might become more forgetful as you get older. Fortunately, memory loss caused by illness or lifestyle factors can often be limited or treated.

Obesity

Roughly one-third of Americans are obese, meaning they have a body mass index (BMI) of 30 or higher (see www.nhlbisupport.com/bmi to calculate your BMI). Being obese leaves you more prone to a host of medical problems—including dementia and Alzheimer's disease, as several studies confirm. So-called central obesity—the classic "spare tire"—in middle age appears to be particularly risky, according to a number of studies. For example, a 2011 observational study that followed 1,459 older New Yorkers, average age 76, for a little under four years found that a bigger waist-to-hip ratio raised the risk of a late-life Alzheimer's diagnosis. This was true even after researchers adjusted for risk factors such as diabetes, heart disease, and the ApoE E4 allele.

In addition, people who are obese face a higher risk of heart disease and diabetes—two conditions that have also been linked to a higher risk of dementia (see below).

Cardiovascular disease and its risk factors

Physicians now know that what's bad for the heart is also bad for the brain. Conditions that have been linked with heart disease—high blood pressure, high cholesterol, and diabetes—have also been linked to memory problems. More and more, research is strengthening the link between injuries to the brain tissue caused by "silent" strokes and the development of symptoms of Alzheimer's disease.

High blood pressure

Adults with high blood pressure (hypertension) are more prone to memory impairment than people with normal blood pressure. Moreover, people with hypertension experience memory loss that is more severe than that suffered by individuals who don't have hypertension. These differences hold true regardless of age.

The link between vascular dementia and hypertension escaped attention for many years because people suffering from dementia often have normal or low blood pressure. But long-term studies now show that blood pressure in midlife may predict brain function years later. One example is the Honolulu-Asia Aging Study, which began in the mid-1960s and evaluated the health of Japanese American men over nearly three decades. The participants' average age was 53 at the beginning of the study and 78 at final evaluation. When the researchers compared performance on cognitive function tests and midlife blood pressure, they found a link between poor mental function late in life and high systolic pressure (the top number of a blood pressure reading) 25 years earlier. Interestingly, the connection was not present for men who had had high blood pressure, but who lowered it by taking medication.

High blood pressure increases dementia by accelerating atherosclerosis, the buildup of plaque in the arteries that impairs circulation. A reduction in circulation can slow blood flow to the brain, which can harm the cells of the brain and cause memory problems. Even worse, if blood flow to one area of the brain is stopped, brain tissue in that area can die. Each incidence of damage—which is actually a tiny stroke—affects such a small area of the brain that symptoms may not be apparent until a substantial amount of tissue has been destroyed. This is a form of vascular dementia (see page 17), which is a well-recognized cause of memory loss in older people. (Also see "Lessons from the Nun Study," page 22.)

Preliminary research has even documented visual evidence of the effects of hypertension on the brain. Using a technology called arterial spin-labeled magnetic resonance imaging, researchers compared the level of cerebral blood flow in people with hypertension, MCI, and Alzheimer's disease to that of people who did not have these conditions. The images revealed that those with high blood pressure and those with Alzheimer's disease both had marked reductions in blood flow to the brain. The group with MCI also showed trends in this direction, although not as severe.

Hypertension appears to impair memory by damaging the brain's white matter. Changes in white matter occur to some degree in virtually everyone over age 60 and contribute to normal age-related memory loss. But damage to white matter is especially prevalent among people with hypertension, according to a report in *The American Journal of Hypertension*. In this study, 60 people with untreated hypertension had the most extensive white-matter abnormalities and performed worst on tests of memory, learning, and other mental functions. And a 2009 study in *Neurology* that involved more than 6,000 people suggested that controlling blood pressure with medication was linked to a lower risk of dementia, especially in people ages 75 and older.

Of note, a recent large epidemiological study of over 800,000 older male patients with cardiovascular disease suggested that treatment with a class of high blood pressure medications called angiotensin-receptor blockers appeared to substantially reduce the risk of developing dementia and lowered the risk of nursing home placement and death in patients with a pre-existing diagnosis of dementia. More research is needed to determine whether similar effects will be found in randomized clinical trials.

High cholesterol

High cholesterol appears to increase the risk for mild cognitive impairment and Alzheimer's disease many years down the road. People with high cholesterol have a higher than average incidence of these two conditions. It's not clear whether high cholesterol leads to memory loss only through increasing the risk of cerebrovascular disease, or whether the crucial factor is excessive LDL (the "bad" cholesterol) or insufficient HDL (the "good" cholesterol). There is some evidence that the generation of harmful amyloid proteins in the brain might depend on cholesterol.

Many large-scale population studies suggest that people who are treated with statins, a class of cholesterol-lowering medications, reap the additional benefit of reducing their risk of Alzheimer's disease and MCI. But other studies failed to find any such benefit from statin use. The difference may reflect when a person started the drug. For example, a recent study looked at 3,069 people 75 years and older, some cognitively healthy and some with MCI. Researchers found that the people who were cognitively healthy and taking statins at the beginning of the study were somewhat protected from developing cognitive decline as the study progressed. However, people who already had MCI who were taking statins were not protected from progressing further in dementia. This study, as well as others on this topic, have some limitations, so more research is needed before doctors start prescribing statins for dementia prevention in people with normal cholesterol levels.

Coronary artery bypass surgery

Some people who undergo coronary artery bypass surgery to treat blocked arteries experience memory loss and problems concentrating for a while after the operation. An often-cited study found that about half of the people who underwent bypass surgery had trouble remembering things or thinking clearly immediately afterward; approximately six months later, about one in four people continued to experience such problems. Why this happens is not clear.

During some bypass surgeries, the heart is stopped and attached to a heart-lung machine, which circulates blood from the heart to the lungs and the rest of the body. One problem with using the heart-lung machine is that when the heart is connected to it, particles of plaque that had been clinging to artery walls can get dislodged and enter the bloodstream. If these particles travel to the brain, they can impede blood flow and lead to memory-impairing damage.

In an effort to avoid this problem, surgeons developed ways to perform coronary artery bypass without using the heart-lung machine. Although there were high hopes that this beating-heart surgery, also called off-pump coronary artery bypass, would abolish post-bypass memory or thinking problems, that hasn't been the case.

Other research suggests that some of the biological processes involved in coronary artery disease also contribute to Alzheimer's disease and other types of dementia—raising the possibility that it is the underlying vascular disease, and not the bypass procedure, that contributes to most cognitive problems.

Researchers continue to look into this issue. In the meantime, if you are preparing for a bypass operation, talk with your surgeon ahead of time about what strategies are available to minimize the chances of post-surgery memory and thinking problems. After the operation, tell your doctor about any problems with attention or concentration you may be having.

Diabetes

Several large studies have documented links between diabetes and cognitive decline. For example, a 2010 study in *Diabetes Care* that measured cognitive function in 2,613 middle-age to elderly people found that over a five-year period, people with type 2 diabetes experienced a decline in cognitive function that was 2.6 times greater than people without the disease.

Scientists think that many factors link diabetes and dementia. The chronic high blood sugar caused by diabetes contributes, possibly because it damages small blood vessels of the brain. In addition, high blood sugar depresses the function of the hippocampus, which, as noted earlier, acquires and consolidates new memories.

The role of insulin, the hormone that transports sugar from the blood into the body's cells—including cells in the brain—is also being examined. In a study that looked at the brain tissue of people who had died in various stages of Alzheimer's disease, people with the most advanced stage of dementia had few insulin receptors in their brains, indicating that the cells were not processing sugar efficiently.

Metabolic syndrome

Some doctors call this the "most common condition you've never heard of." It affects almost 50 million Americans, yet many of them don't know it. Metabolic syndrome isn't just one condition; it's a combination of problems. You have metabolic syndrome if you have three or more of the following:

• high blood pressure

• excess belly fat, meaning a waist size of 40 inches or more for men, or 35 inches or more for women

• high triglycerides, a kind of blood fat often checked with cholesterol levels

• low high-density lipoprotein (HDL) cholesterol

• high fasting blood sugar.

Lessons from the Nun Study

The Nun Study, an ongoing research project begun in 1986, seeks to understand the hows and whys of aging and Alzheimer's disease. It features a unique population of 678 retired Catholic sisters, all of whom agreed to donate their brains at death. The unprecedented wealth of information available about the sisters' personal and medical histories, combined with the relative uniformity of their lifestyles, allowed researchers to tease out some of the medical and social factors that put an individual at risk for developing dementia.

One of the most significant findings has been the understanding of how cardiovascular factors interact with Alzheimer's disease pathology. The women in the study who seemed to fare the best cognitively were those whose brains showed little evidence of stroke, even if they had brain damage consistent with moderate Alzheimer's. From this, researchers conclude that a healthy brain has reserve capacity it can draw on to maintain normal functions even when Alzheimer's disease is present. On the other hand, when the brain is compromised by cardiovascular disease, dementia symptoms appear at an earlier stage.

Metabolic syndrome puts you at greater risk for a host of other problems, including stroke, diabetes, and fatal heart attack. A study published in the February 8, 2011 issue of the journal *Neurology* suggests that memory loss can also be added to that list. The observational study found that of the 7,087 French people who took part, about 16% had metabolic syndrome. Over the four years of the study, the people took several memory tests, and those who had metabolic syndrome were 20% more likely than others to have a decline in overall memory. The people with metabolic syndrome were also much more likely to have a declining memory if they had one of three specific problems found on the metabolic syndrome list, namely, diabetes, high triglyceride levels, or a low HDL level.

Depression

The relationship between depression and memory loss is complex. Depression can be a cause as well as an effect of memory dysfunction. Depression also seems to put people at risk for later Alzheimer's disease—risk goes up the more episodes of depression a person has in his or her lifetime. In itself, severe, ongoing, and untreated depression can make people forgetful by interfering with their ability to concentrate and process information. This is particularly true in the elderly. In fact, doctors coined the term "depressive pseudo-dementia" to describe elderly patients with severe memory impairment based on depression. Once the depression is treated, the patient's memory can return to the level of function that existed before he or she was depressed.

However, especially if a person is clinically depressed for the first time at an old age, the depression often is a very early manifestation of neurodegenerative disease. In such people, treatment of depression may improve mood and cognition, but only temporarily. Thus, older people who develop late-life depression need to be closely monitored.

Although depression can be a symptom of early Alzheimer's disease, there are key differences in the memory loss experienced by people suffering from depression alone and people experiencing depression in conjunction with Alzheimer's. In people with depression alone, cognitive function usually fluctuates with mood. When mood improves—usually in response to treatment with medication, psychotherapy, or both—cognitive function generally improves as well. By contrast, someone with Alzheimer's disease will continue to have impaired cognitive functioning even when the depression lifts.

Hearing loss

It makes sense: if you have trouble hearing something, you're bound to have trouble remembering it. One study found that adults with mild to moderate hearing loss remembered fewer of the items from a list of 15 spoken words than did adults with good hearing. The researchers concluded that the extra effort involved in trying to hear the words diverted brain resources from acquisition and consolidation of memory. Hearing loss is a remarkably common problem, particularly in the elderly. Periodic hearing tests should be part of routine medical care.

It is also highly treatable. Hearing aid technology has improved greatly. If you have tried a hearing aid in the past and didn't find it helpful, consider trying again. Note that successful use of a hearing aid may require several follow-up visits to the hearing aid specialist, who will fine-tune and adjust the device for your needs.

Hormones

Many naturally occurring hormones can affect memory and overall cognitive function. Three of these hormones—estrogen, testosterone, and thyroid hormone—have been widely studied with regard to their effects on memory.

Estrogen

Many women experience trouble with memory during menopause, when their levels of estrogen fall sharply. However, stress or other psychological issues, sleep disturbance due to hot flashes, or a combination of factors could also be to blame.

Some studies suggest that estrogen protects neurons, which might explain a connection with memory. If that's true, hormone supplements should protect against age-related memory difficulties. However, a number of studies have revealed the opposite, casting doubt on estrogen's promise for preserving memory. Still, ongoing research is looking into whether different forms of estrogen given at different times (for example, during perimenopause) may prove beneficial. Much study is needed before this hypothesis is proved one way or the other, but studies are starting to trickle in. For example, one study of medical records of female members of the Kaiser Permanente health maintenance organization found that women who took hormone replacement therapy only at midlife had a 26% lower risk of having dementia, whereas those who took the hormone supplements later than midlife had a 48% higher risk.

Testosterone

Men with high levels of testosterone have better visual and verbal memories than men with low levels. Still, the value of testosterone supplementation in older men is controversial. One early study found that testosterone supplements led to improvements in working memory in men. Then in 2006, a review paper reported that some randomized controlled trials—the gold standard of medical studies—found that testosterone replacement improved certain types of brain functions in older men. This was true in men with and without low levels of testosterone, and with and without dementia or MCI. The researchers noted, however, that many of the studies were small and therefore further study is needed. In contrast, a 2007 study of healthy older men found no such benefit. It should be noted, too, that testosterone supplements have drawbacks—they can increase the risk of some kinds of cancer and may also raise the risk for stroke and for vascular dementia. In addition, the type of testosterone and the amount (if any) that should be given as a treatment for memory problems still needs to be established.

Thyroid hormone

The thyroid gland secretes hormones that control metabolism, the rate at which the body burns energy.

When the thyroid doesn't function properly, it can release too much or too little of these hormones, making the metabolism run too fast or too slow. Either problem can interfere with learning and memory. Hyperthyroidism, which causes an abnormally fast metabolism, can make people feel confused. Hypothyroidism, which causes an abnormally slow metabolism, can make people feel sluggish, sleepy, and depressed. Research on animals shows that changes in the levels of thyroid hormone cause physiological changes in the hippocampus. Research also shows that when thyroid problems are treated, people's memory problems diminish.

Medications

Many over-the-counter and prescription drugs have side effects that can scramble thinking and dim memory. Older people tend to be more sensitive to these effects. Moreover, older people often take multiple medications. Although one drug alone may not cause problems, the cumulative effect of several drugs may make it difficult to carry out basic daily activities such as bathing, dressing, and even walking.

Popular over-the-counter drugs with these side effects—often listed on the label as dry mouth, blurred vision, and confused thinking—include antihistamines used to treat allergies, colds, and coughs. There are literally dozens of these products lining drugstore shelves; check the ingredient list for brompheniramine, chlorpheniramine, and diphenhydramine, all of which have these side effects. Doctors sometimes recommend that people take diphenhydramine (better known by its trade name, Benadryl) to help them fall asleep. In fact, diphenhydramine is also the main ingredient in many over-the-counter sleep aids, such as Compoz, Sominex, and Unisom, as well as Tylenol PM.

Among prescription drugs, the prime culprits include certain ones used to treat depression, such as amitriptyline (Elavil) and nortriptyline (Aventyl, Pamelor); overactive bladder, such as oxybutynin (Ditropan, Urotrol, and other brands); and heartburn, such as cimetidine (Tagamet).

Table 2 Medications that may affect memory and possible substitutes

IF YOU TAKE ...	...ASK ABOUT SWITCHING TO ONE OF THESE DRUGS
paroxetine (Paxil)	another SSRI, such as fluoxetine (Prozac) or sertraline (Zoloft), or a drug from the SNRI class (Cymbalta, Effexor, others)
cimetidine (Tagamet)	a proton-pump inhibitor (Prevacid, Prilosec, Nexium, others)
oxybutynin (Ditropan) or **tolterodine** (Detrol, Detrusitol)	trospium (Sanctura), solifenacin (Vesicare), or darifenacin (Enablex) which are anticholinergic but more selective for the bladder
amitriptyline (Elavil), **desipramine** (Norpramin), or **nortriptyline** (Aventyl, Pamelor)	a wide range of alternatives, depending on your reason for taking a tricyclic antidepressant (neuropathic pain, depression, etc.)
captopril (Capoten)	a different ACE inhibitor
cold or allergy medication containing brompheniramine, chlorpheniramine, or diphenhydramine	loratadine (Claritin) or another non-sedating antihistamine

These medications share a common mechanism: blocking the neurotransmitter acetylcholine, which is why they are known as anticholinergic drugs. Certain drugs used to treat Alzheimer's disease, such as donepezil (Aricept), have the exact opposite effect—they boost levels of acetylcholine in the brain. So it makes sense to steer clear of anticholinergics when possible. One study reported that the use of medications with anticholinergic activity was linked to a more rapid decline in the cognitive performance of older adults who had been studied an average of 7.8 years.

If you've noticed any kind of confusion or thinking problems since starting a new medication, ask your doctor about a possible substitute, which is often (but not always) possible. For some potential alternatives to drugs with anticholinergic actions, see Table 2. ▼

10 ways of life to promote memory health

The way you live, what you eat and drink, and how you treat your body can affect your memory. Here are 10 steps you can take to improve your health—and your memory, mostly by protecting it from the risk of decline.

1. Exercise

Physical fitness and mental fitness go together. People who engage in regular vigorous exercise also tend to stay mentally sharp into their 70s and 80s. Researchers don't know precisely how much exercise is needed for good brain health. The available research suggests that the exercise needn't be extreme, but should be moderately vigorous and regular. The people in the landmark MacArthur Foundation Study on Successful Aging whose mental functions remained strong were active almost daily. A study from Case Western Reserve University School of Medicine concluded that individuals who exercised—by walking or by engaging in physically active hobbies, such as gardening—had a lower risk for Alzheimer's disease. See "Exercise recommendations for older adults," below, for the federal guidelines.

Supporting the connection between exercise and cognitive health are findings from a number of studies, including the following:

- An analysis of more than 13,000 women participating in the long-running Nurses' Health Study found that women who reported getting the most exercise at age 60 were almost twice as likely to become "successful survivors" compared with those who were the most sedentary. Successful survivors were women who lived beyond age 70 without developing cognitive, physical, or mental health limitations or a major chronic health problem. How much movement bestows this benefit? The equivalent of walking briskly for five to six hours per week.

- Researchers at the University of Pittsburgh recruited 120 adults, ages 55 to 80, and randomly assigned them to one of two groups. One group walked briskly for 40 minutes per day, three times a week, while the other performed stretching exercises for the same amount of time. One year later, participants in both groups had improved on memory tests, but the walking group showed more improvement than the stretching group. Brain scans taken at the start of the study and one year later revealed that the hippocampus grew by 2% in the walkers but shrank by 1.4% in the people who did stretching exercises. This latter statistic sounds alarming, but a reduction of that degree is actually normal in older people. That said, the larger the hippocampus—whether the participant was assigned to walking or stretching—the better his or her score on the memory test.

- Researchers queried 3,903 men and women ages 55 and older about their exercise habits. After two years, they found that people who said they exercised at a

---

Exercise recommendations for older adults

If you're 65 years of age or older, are generally fit, and have no limiting health conditions, you can follow the guidelines listed below, which will deliver benefits for your body as well as your brain. If you have a health condition that limits your activity, do as much as you are able to do comfortably and safely. Always check with your doctor before starting an exercise program.

- Two hours and 30 minutes (150 minutes) of moderate-intensity aerobic activity (e.g., brisk walking) every week

  or

- one hour and 15 minutes (75 minutes) of vigorous-intensity aerobic activity (i.e., jogging or running) every week

  or

- an equivalent mix of moderate- and vigorous-intensity aerobic activity

  and

- muscle-strengthening activities on two or more days a week that work all major muscle groups (legs, hips, back, abdomen, chest, shoulders, and arms).

moderate level (less than three times a week) or a high level (three or more times a week) were half as likely to have developed dementia compared with those who got no exercise.

- Older men who walked less than a quarter-mile per day were 1.8 times more likely to develop dementia compared with those who walked more than two miles a day. The findings, from the Honolulu-Asia Aging Study, were based on more than 2,000 physically able men between the ages of 71 and 93 and published in *The Journal of the American Medical Association* in 2004.

- Vigorous leisure activity for just 20 to 30 minutes twice a week at midlife was linked to a lower risk of dementia an average of 21 years later, according to a 2005 study of more than 1,400 adults.

- In 2006, a six-year study of 1,740 adults ages 65 and older reported that people who exercised more than three times a week had a lower risk of dementia than their sedentary counterparts (see Figure 6).

Exercise may help memory in several ways. First of all, exercise helps reduce the risk for diabetes, high cholesterol, high blood pressure, and stroke—diseases that can lead to memory loss. Second, it's good for the lungs, and people who have good lung function are sending a higher volume of oxygen through their blood vessels and into their brains. There is also some evidence that exercise leads to increased connections between brain cells and enhances neurotransmitter function in humans. Finally, animal research has shown that exercise increases the level of neurotrophins, substances that nourish brain cells and help protect them against damage from stroke and other injuries.

Experts recommend that you build physical activity into your daily routine. Here are some examples:

- When possible, walk instead of driving.
- Set aside time each day for exercise—for example, a brisk half-hour walk around the neighborhood. For motivation, ask your spouse or a friend to go with you.
- Use the stairs instead of the elevator.
- Exercise at home, possibly with an exercise video.

Keep trim. Exercise and watch what you eat to make sure you maintain a healthy weight. This lowers your risk for illnesses such as diabetes and hypertension, which can impair your memory.

- Plant a garden.
- Take an exercise class or join a health club.
- Swim regularly, if you have access to a pool or beach.
- Learn a sport that requires modest physical exertion, such as tennis.

2. Eat a Mediterranean-style diet

The Mediterranean diet highlights whole grains, fruits and vegetables, and healthy fats from fish, nuts, and healthy oils. This eating style helps promote heart health and may also lessen the risk of cognitive problems later in life, according to several studies. One, which followed more than 2,000 people over four years, found that the more closely a person followed the diet, the lower the risk of probable Alzheimer's disease. Similarly, a subsequent study suggested that closer adherence to a Mediterranean-style diet also reduced the risk of people with mild cognitive impairment converting to dementia. It's not clear

Figure 6 Getting regular exercise helps fend off dementia

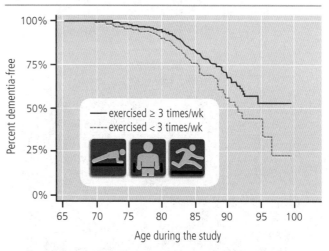

People who exercise three times a week or more are less likely to develop dementia (13 per 1,000) than people who exercise less than three times per week (20 per 1,000).
Adapted from Larson EB, et al., *Annals of Internal Medicine* (Jan. 17, 2006), Vol. 144, No. 2, pp. 73–81.

whether the benefits resulted from the diminished risk of heart disease and stroke associated with the Mediterranean diet or some other mechanism. A limitation of these studies is that they are not randomized controlled trials, so factors other than diet may be driving the effects.

The Consensus Statement on Preventing Alzheimer's Disease and Cognitive Decline issued by the National Institutes of Health in 2010 gave a thumbs-up to one particular component of the Mediterranean diet—fish. The consensus statement said that among nutritional factors, "the most consistent evidence is available for longer chain omega-3 fatty acids (often measured as fish consumption)." Evidence that supports the connection between brain health and omega-3s includes data from the Framingham Heart Study. This study revealed that people with initially higher blood levels of the omega-3 fatty acid docosahexaenoic acid (DHA) had lower rates of dementia over a period of nine years.

Other components of the diet have also been shown to prevent dementia. For example, eating large

What about vitamins?

Despite some initial evidence that specific vitamins might prevent or treat memory problems, studies to test their potential have proved disappointing, as described in the following summaries.

B vitamins. Three B vitamins—B_6, B_{12}, and folic acid—help break down homocysteine, an amino acid released during digestion. High levels of homocysteine are linked with the development of both cardiovascular disease and Alzheimer's disease. People were hopeful that taking these B vitamins would also work as a treatment. Preliminary research published in 2010 showed a lower rate of atrophy (wasting away) of brain tissue in MCI patients older than 70 who took a combination of B vitamins—B_{12}, B_6, and folic acid—versus those taking a placebo. People with MCI who go on to convert to dementia often have accelerated rates of atrophy, so the researchers note that further research is needed to see if treatment with B vitamins actually stops or slows this conversion.

However, other studies do not shine such a positive light on the B vitamins. For example, a review by the Cochrane Collaboration, an international group of independent experts, found that in three of four carefully designed trials, vitamin B supplements did nothing to slow disease progression in patients with either dementia or MCI.

It's possible that by the time dementia or cognitive impairment becomes apparent, the underlying pathology has already progressed to the point that vitamin supplementation may no longer help. But the Cochrane reviewers also reported that three of four studies conducted in healthy older people found that vitamin B supplements were no more effective than placebo at protecting cognition and slowing age-related decline.

Vitamin E. Vitamin E is an antioxidant that counters the effects of free radicals—naturally occurring but highly reactive molecules that can damage cells. Research in animals suggests that brain cell damage by free radicals may contribute not only to age-related cognitive decline but also to MCI or Alzheimer's. Studies in people, meanwhile, have found that abnormally low blood levels of vitamin E are associated with impaired cognitive functioning and Alzheimer's.

Although one early study indicated a benefit from high doses of vitamin E supplements in people with Alzheimer's disease, subsequent findings reduced enthusiasm for this supplement because they didn't show that it had the same efficacy for preventing the disease. For example, research has found that vitamin E did not lower the risk of developing Alzheimer's dementia in patients with MCI. A 2009 study reported that neither vitamin E nor vitamin C, beta carotene, or combinations of the three slowed cognitive decline among women who already had heart disease or were at risk for it.

Today, most experts recommend that people take no more than 400 IU of vitamin E a day. Higher amounts may increase the risk of death from various causes, according to a 2004 report that pooled data from a number of studies. If you have a bleeding disorder or are taking anticoagulant medications such as aspirin, talk with your doctor before taking vitamin E supplements in any amount. Vitamin E can be dangerous because it promotes bleeding.

- Vitamin B_{12} deficiency can mimic some of the symptoms of Alzheimer's disease and other types of dementia by causing disorientation and confusion. People can prevent or treat a vitamin B_{12} deficiency by taking supplements or eating fortified foods. People who complain of memory or thinking difficulties should have a blood test to rule out a vitamin B_{12} deficiency, since it is often treatable.

- About 6% of people ages 60 and older are deficient in vitamin B_{12}, and nearly 20% are borderline deficient. Elderly people produce less stomach acid than younger people, which makes it harder for them to metabolize this vitamin from food sources.

amounts of unsaturated fat—which includes fish oil as well as most vegetable oils—reduces risk, according to some studies. In one study, which looked at a subset of the famed Women's Health Initiative, 482 women ages 60 and older were observed for three years. They reported on their diets, and researchers tested their memory and other cognitive skills at the beginning of the study and at the end. When the women were classified according to how much monounsaturated fat they consumed, those who ate the most had significantly less memory decline than those who ate less monounsaturated fat. In the highest consumption group, monounsaturated fat made up at least 13.27% of dietary calories.

Eating a lot of fruits and vegetables can be especially beneficial because many are good sources of vitamins and other nutrients that may protect against diseases and age-related deterioration throughout the body.

3. If you drink alcohol, do so moderately

Excessive alcohol use increases the risk for memory loss and dementia. People with alcoholism have difficulty performing short-term memory tasks, such as memorizing lists. Another type of memory loss associated with alcohol use is called Korsakoff's syndrome, in which severe amnesia comes on suddenly and dramatically as a result of long-term vitamin B_1 (thiamine) deficiency combined with the toxic effects of alcohol on the brain. The memory loss of Korsakoff's syndrome is permanent about a quarter of the time, but it can be reversible to a lesser or greater degree in most cases, especially if it is caught early. Other alcohol-related memory problems may be reversible if the person sharply cuts down on drinking and eats a healthy diet.

Moderate drinking, on the other hand, may actually improve one's ability to remember. For example, a 2011 study looked at 922 healthy adults, all about 70 years old. Because they had participated in an earlier study, their IQs had been tracked since they were age 11. The researchers found that those who drank more than two alcoholic drinks per day did better on cognitive tests than those who didn't drink or who drank two or fewer drinks per day. However—

and this is a big however—after the researchers adjusted for childhood IQ and adult social class, the strength of the links between drinking and cognition decreased. A small association still existed between memory and alcohol intake in both women and men, and alcohol intake and verbal ability in women only.

Other studies have linked moderate drinking with a reduced risk of Alzheimer's disease. Some studies suggest that red wine in particular (as opposed to other forms of alcohol) may have an especially salutary effect, possibly due to resveratrol, a compound found in the skin of red grapes that has garnered attention as an anti-aging compound. A number of studies in mice suggest that resveratrol has brain-protecting abilities, but its potential benefit in humans remains to be determined. Alcohol may be memory-protective because of its antioxidant properties and the fact that it decreases the risk of non-hemorrhagic stroke.

Clearly, many questions remain about the relationship between alcohol and memory. Experts caution that even though research is mounting in support of the biological benefits of alcohol on memory, it's still better to forgo alcohol altogether than to over-imbibe.

4. Keep learning

Over time, people who don't challenge their minds exhibit a greater degree of memory decline compared with people who remain mentally active. The MacArthur aging study found that education level was the strongest predictor of mental capacity as people aged. A study in the *Journal of Gerontology: Psychological Sciences* reported that people who held jobs that involved complex work, such as speaking to, instructing, or negotiating with others, had a lower risk of dementia than people whose jobs were less intellectually demanding.

Most experts think it's not the years of formal education or the type of occupation per se that benefits memory. Instead, a lifelong habit of learning and engaging in mentally challenging activities seems to keep the brain in shape.

Scientists believe that intellectual enrichment and learning stimulate the brain to make more connections, increasing the density of synapses. As a result, the "educated brain" may possess greater reserves of cognitive ability—a deeper well, so to speak—and be able to sustain more neuronal loss.

Exercising your brain with challenging activities is believed to stimulate communication between brain cells. Some ways of challenging your mind are obvious—for example, doing crossword puzzles, reading, participating in a book discussion group, playing chess, or taking classes. But you don't have to go to great lengths to find mental stimulation. Mental challenges also come from the unexpected occurrences that take you out of your daily routines and make you think. If you're still working, chances are that you get some of these curveballs thrown at you from time to time. But if you aren't working and your time is largely unscheduled, you may need to actively seek out novel experiences and learning opportunities. Planning day trips or longer vacations, meeting regularly with friends and acquaintances, going to the theater or to museums, or just making a point of varying your routine can help keep your mind active and engaged. You can also try cooking new recipes, joining a club, picking up a musical instrument, or learning a new art or craft.

The following studies offer evidence for this phenomenon:

- The more often people read, played games such as cards or checkers, went to museums, or did similar activities, the less likely they were to develop symptoms of Alzheimer's disease, according to a study of 801 elderly people who were followed for an average of 4.5 years.

- In a study of more than 5,000 Chinese men and women, mentally stimulating leisure activities—mainly reading and playing mah-jongg—were associated with a lower risk of developing cognitive impairment.

- Studies have also found an association between an increased participation in stimulating leisure activities at midlife and a decreased risk of developing dementia many decades later.

In 2010, the National Institutes of Health convened a state-of-the-science conference on preventing Alzheimer's and cognitive decline. The resulting consensus statement said that physical activity and cognitive engagement were promising ways to prevent cognitive decline.

5. Manage your stress

Several studies link stress to memory loss. The minor stresses of daily life, like deadline pressures or petty arguments, aren't the issue here; the problem is an ongoing sense of extreme anxiety. Such severe stress may impair a person's memory. Some people—for example, veterans of wars or others who experience profoundly traumatic events—may develop post-traumatic stress disorder (PTSD), a condition in which intrusive memories of the traumatic event recur persistently and cause the individual to experience episodes of sustained, severe anxiety.

Prolonged or frequently elevated levels of the stress hormone cortisol (as seen in PTSD) can harm brain structures vital to memory. Through animal research, scientists have discovered that cortisol damages neurons in the hippocampus. Brain imaging studies reveal that the hippocampus may sustain damage or shrink in people with PTSD.

One study implicated cortisol in memory dysfunction in humans as well. In the study, a group of healthy adults received daily low-dose treatments of cortisol over the course of four consecutive days—about the amount that would be released under everyday stress. Another group received high doses over the same period of time. All participants took a test in which they listened to stories and then had to remember details about them immediately and 30 minutes later. People who had received the higher cortisol dose remembered less, both immediately and later, than people receiving the lower dose.

The memory dysfunction induced by this four-day experiment was reversible; once the cortisol wore off, the participants' memories returned to normal. No one knows how many days, weeks, months, or years of high-level stress it takes to cause irreversible memory impairment. What we do know is that a stressful event will cause some people to react more intensely than others, and it is the resulting long-term stress reaction that does the damage. To that extent, people may be able to control the harm that stress does to the memory by trying to modify their exposure and responses to stressful life events.

One way to reduce stress is to work on gaining a greater sense of control over your life. The MacArthur Foundation's study on aging found that the people who reported the most "self-efficacy," or mastery, also had the best memory in old age. The researchers viewed self-efficacy as a buffer against the feeling of helplessness that often contributes to stress.

There's no one-size-fits-all strategy for reducing stress. You have to find strategies that work for you. For some people, trying to reappraise the situation in more positive terms or gathering support from friends and family can be effective. For others, taking a brisk walk or getting other kinds of regular exercise helps. Listening to music, talking to a friend, socializing, or engaging in a relaxing activity, such as gardening, knitting, or meditating, can also help you cope with stressful situations (see "Meditating changes your brain," at right). If you can't lower your stress level on your own, you might benefit from counseling.

6. Get a good night's sleep

People who don't sleep well at night tend to be more forgetful than people who sleep soundly. A good night's sleep is essential for consolidating memories. Although people vary in their need for sleep, six hours may be the minimum that older adults need to ensure adequate daytime alertness and memory function (see "Sleep, perchance to remember," page 32).

Sleep may aid memory in another way as well—by lowering levels of stress hormones. Stress hormones decline during the first few hours of sleep, which experts believe may free up the hippocampus to consolidate memories.

With age, people become more prone to sleep disorders. The most common sleep disorder is insomnia, which is difficulty falling asleep or staying asleep. Unfortunately, many medicines used in the treatment of insomnia can also impair memory and general cognitive function, and it's best to avoid long-term use of sleep-inducing medications.

The following practices can help with insomnia:

▶ Meditating changes your brain

Mindfulness meditation is the practice of paying attention to what you're experiencing from moment to moment, without drifting into thoughts about the past or concerns about the future, and without analyzing (or making judgments about) what is going on around you. Generally, meditation is associated with changing stress levels. Now, a small study that used magnetic resonance imaging to examine brain structures showed that meditation changes the brain, too.

Researchers at Massachusetts General Hospital in Boston and the University of Massachusetts Medical School in Worcester found that meditating alters regions of the brain associated with memory, awareness of self, and compassion. Another small study suggests that meditation can improve memory in people with Alzheimer's.

We already know that learning new physical skills (such as juggling) can change the brain; this study offers intriguing new evidence that learning to think in a new way can do the same.

- Establish and maintain a consistent sleep schedule and routine. Go to bed at the same time each night and wake up at the same time each morning. A set sleep routine will "train" you to fall asleep and wake up more easily.

- Use the bed only for sleep and sex.

- Plan to do your most vigorous exercise early in the day. Exercising in the hours immediately before bedtime causes physiological changes that may interfere with sleep. Exercising in the morning, on the other hand, enhances your alertness when you need it most—at the beginning of the day.

- Avoid coffee and other sources of caffeine (e.g., chocolate, many soft drinks, some brands of pain relievers, many types of tea) after midmorning, because caffeine is a stimulant that can keep you awake for hours.

- Avoid excessive napping during the daytime. Prolonged napping can disrupt your natural sleep cycle and prevent you from feeling tired enough to fall asleep at night.

- Don't take sleeping pills unless nothing else works. If you do take a prescription sleep medicine, work with your doctor on using it effectively, but only on a short-term basis, because sleep medications can be habit-forming. In addition, like sleep deprivation, sleeping pills can cause memory loss.

- Some people find that drinking warm milk before bedtime helps them feel sleepy. Milk contains tryptophan, a chemical that may help you relax.
- Don't try to sleep if you're not tired; otherwise you'll set yourself up for tossing and turning. If you're still awake after about 20 minutes in bed, get up and read awhile to help yourself relax.

If you experience persistent sleep problems, consult your physician so that you can identify the specific issues and get the necessary treatment.

Another common disorder is obstructive sleep apnea (OSA), in which interrupted breathing can interrupt sleep with hundreds of "mini-awakenings" each night. More than 18 million American adults have sleep apnea, with more men than women being affected by it. It becomes more prevalent with age, affecting at least one in 10 people older than 65. It causes loud snoring and gasping for air. If you have OSA, treating the problem appears to improve some aspects of cognitive function in people both with and without dementia, according to several studies.

7. Stop smoking

Smokers have a greater degree of age-related memory loss and other memory problems than nonsmokers. For example, in a large and racially diverse study done in the United States, participants voluntarily completed a health survey during routine medical visits between 1978 and 1985, when they were 50 to 60 years old. During this initial assessment, clinicians measured blood pressure, cholesterol levels, weight, and other factors that contribute to heart disease. Participants answered questions, including how many packs of cigarettes they smoked per day. The researchers then examined medical records for 21,123 participants still alive between 1994 and 2008 (an average of 23 years after the first assessments) to determine who developed Alzheimer's or another dementia.

They found that 5,367 people (roughly a quarter of the sample) were diagnosed with some type of dementia, including 1,136 with Alzheimer's. After adjusting for age, gender, race, education, and cardiac risk factors, the researchers found that people who had smoked more than two packs of cigarettes a day at midlife had more than double the risk of developing dementia in old age when compared with nonsmokers. However, people who had stopped smoking by midlife and those who had smoked less than half a pack a day had a risk of dementia similar to that of people who had never smoked.

Sleep, perchance to remember

Why does sleep make a difference to memory? One theory suggests that changes in brain activity during two phases of sleep—slow-wave sleep and rapid-eye-movement (REM) sleep—are important for memory consolidation. Research with rodents showed that during slow-wave sleep, the pattern of activity in the hippocampus was very similar to the pattern that appeared earlier when the animals were engaged in learning something. This finding suggests that during slow-wave sleep, the hippocampus "replays" the recently acquired information to strengthen the neuronal patterns that were activated during the acquisition phase. This replaying of the learning scenario is the key component of the consolidation process.

An interesting study published in the March 2007 issue of *Science* elaborates on this theory. Research participants played a memory game called Concentration, in which they were asked to recall the locations of similar cards. Each time a person matched a pair of cards correctly, he or she was exposed to the scent of roses. Later that night, the rose fragrance was reintroduced during slow-wave sleep for half of the participants. The next morning, these individuals demonstrated a greater ability to match the locations of previously learned pairs over the subjects who did not receive sleep-time exposure to the scent. These results can be explained, the researchers say, by the fact that the rose scent activated the hippocampus and provided contextual information that aided in the consolidation of the memory and completing the learning task.

Research has also revealed that important changes take place in the brain during REM sleep, which is the time when dreaming occurs. In particular, there is increased activity in the cortex during dreams. Some scientists now think that dreaming is one of the ways in which the brain strengthens the neuronal pathways that encode memories.

Research also shows that smokers are less adept at recalling names and faces. A British study reported that the verbal memory function of people ages 43 to 53 was weaker in the smokers than in the nonsmokers. A study published in *Neurology* tracked the memory of 9,209 people ages 65 and older annually for several years by giving them the Mini–Mental State Examination, a standard test of cognitive functions. Nearly everyone's score dropped during this period, but the decline was five times greater for smokers than for people who never smoked. These conclusions were confirmed in a 2007 meta-analysis of 19 studies involving a total of more than 26,000 participants. Smokers showed a greater yearly decline in cognitive scores compared with nonsmokers. In addition, current smokers exhibited a higher risk of Alzheimer's disease than did former smokers.

Smoking increases the risk for vascular diseases, stroke, and hypertension, all potential causes of memory impairment. No one knows whether smoking directly impairs memory or is merely associated with memory loss because it causes disorders that contribute to poorer brain function.

Regardless of the exact nature of the link between smoking and memory loss, if you smoke, it pays to quit. Research shows that people who stop smoking have less cognitive decline than people who continue to smoke. That said, quitting isn't easy. Most people need help, in the form of counseling, nicotine replacement therapy, or medications.

8. Say no to illicit drugs

People who use certain illicit drugs are likely to have problems with memory and related cognitive functions—not only while they are under the influence, but also for weeks after the drugs' immediate effects wear off.

There's no question that recreational use of marijuana produces short-term problems with thinking, working memory, and executive function. Marijuana's active chemical, THC, causes its psychoactive effect by attaching to receptors in brain regions vital for memory formation, including the hippocampus, amygdala, and cerebral cortex. There's debate about whether long-term use of marijuana (either for medical or recreational purposes) produces persistent cognitive problems. Although early studies of recreational users reported such difficulties, the studies had key design problems. Typically they compared long-term marijuana smokers with people who had never used the drug, without controlling for characteristics such as education or cognitive functioning. These factors might play a part in determining who chooses to smoke marijuana long-term and who never tries it, as well as who might be most at risk for thinking and memory problems later on. That said, studies suggest that although overall cognitive ability remains intact, long-term use of marijuana may cause subtle but lasting impairments in executive function.

Memory impairment is also a side effect of habitual cocaine use. Cocaine users score lower than nonusers on tests of working memory and recall of long-term memories. Deficits are apparent on tests of verbal memory, even after users have abstained from cocaine for 45 days.

One of the worst things you can do to your memory is to use illicit drugs. It is unclear how much of the memory impairment can be restored by quitting, but at the very least, quitting can prevent further damage.

9. Protect your brain from injury and toxins

Head trauma is a major cause of memory impairment and appears to be a risk factor for future development of dementia. You can reduce the risk of head trauma by using the appropriate gear during high-speed activities and contact sports.

Wear seat belts when riding in motor vehicles. Car accidents are by far the most common cause of brain injury, and wearing seat belts greatly reduces the injury risk. Wear a helmet when bicycling, riding on a motorcycle, in-line skating, and skiing.

Lead, mercury, and other chemicals present in homes and workplaces can cause memory loss and poor concentration. Lead poisoning can result from drinking contaminated tap water and breathing in lead dust generated by the deterioration of lead paint in homes built before 1978, when it was outlawed. Carbon monoxide fumes leak from malfunctioning household furnaces and are spewed from automobile exhaust systems. Mercury and other toxic substances are found in some paints, dyes, and inks used in artwork. Still other sources of toxic exposure are pesticides used in home gardens and farms, darkroom chemicals, and chemicals used in metalwork and woodwork.

Reduce your exposure to toxic substances by taking sensible precautions. Before using paints, solvents, and pesticides, read the labels for safe handling. Test your home water supply and use a water filter to eliminate lead, if necessary. Avoid sanding, scraping, and otherwise disrupting lead paint on older homes. If you do plan to remove lead paint, hire a government-approved contractor for this work. Have your car and furnace serviced regularly to minimize carbon monoxide emissions. All this said, keep in mind that illicit drugs and heavy alcohol use pose much greater danger to the brain than these chemicals.

10. Stay socially active

Close ties with others can improve the cognitive performance of older people, according to the MacArthur study on aging and other research. Social support can come from relationships with friends, relatives, or caregivers, as well as from a religious community or other organized group.

A 2008 study of 3,610 people between the ages of 24 and 96 looked at the relationship between participants' mental function and their level of social contact based on how often they talked on the phone to friends, neighbors, and relatives. The researchers found that the higher the individual's level of social interaction, the better his or her mental function; this result was found across all age groups. A second study by the same team compared the cognitive effects of 10 minutes of group discussion against a similar amount of time spent in solitary intellectual activities such as silent reading or crossword puzzles. When tested on mental processing speed and working memory, the group that engaged in social interaction performed better.

There are several ways that social engagement may benefit your memory. Intellectually stimulating activities often go hand in hand with social interaction. Social relationships can also provide support during stressful times, reducing the damaging effects that stress can have on the brain.

A meaningful, socially engaging activity may prove especially helpful, as evidenced by a study conducted with the Baltimore Experience Corps, in which 149 older people were assigned to either a wait-list control group or a group that helps elementary school children to read, use the library, and behave in class for 15 hours a week during the school year. Early results suggest that participants remained engaged in the program for many months and improved their executive function and memory. ♥

Improving everyday memory

Although there is no miracle drug for people with normal age-related memory loss, there are plenty of specific techniques you can learn to improve your ability to retain new information and skills. Doctors and other clinicians who work with people to improve their cognitive performance and memory have found these strategies to be very effective. They aren't difficult to master. Indeed, many are simple things that you probably do already, but can benefit from doing more regularly. In other words, make an investment of time to reap the rewards of a sharper, quicker mind.

These techniques fall into three general categories: organizational tools, behavioral strategies, and memory-enhancing techniques that make new information meaningful and relevant to you, thus making it easier to remember.

Organizational tools

Most people need to organize a multitude of facts each day: dates and locations of appointments, people's names and phone numbers, even where they left the car keys. Information that is well organized is much easier to learn and remember. There are many organizational tools, including time-honored ones such as address books and calendars, as well as electronic organizers that beep to remind you when it's time to do something. It doesn't matter which tool you choose; what matters is that you use it consistently.

Here's a brief list of the types of information that people often forget and some organizational strategies to help you remember. (Also see Table 3.)

Belongings. Have a designated spot for your most important personal belongings (keys, glasses, handbag) and always put them there when you're not using them.

Meetings and appointments. Maintain a calendar (on paper, on your cell phone, or using an electronic pocket organizer) in which you write appointments and important dates, and keep it with you at all times. For people who don't use electronic organizers, some experts recommend a "memory notebook," which is a binder that has a weekly calendar and paper for writing down important information. Develop the habit of checking your organizer or notebook at least several times each day.

Daily tasks. In addition to listing your appointments, keep a list of the miscellaneous things that you have to do each day or week—people to call, items you need to buy, routine maintenance on your car or home, and so on. Keep those to-do lists in your electronic organizer or memory notebook.

Contact information. Keep your address book or electronic organizer up to date with the names and phone numbers of friends, relatives, and professionals or companies with whom you do business (bank, doctors, mechanic, etc.).

Vital information. Keep important documents like insurance papers and medical records in a file cabinet or other designated location. Record other vital information in your

WHAT YOU FORGET	HOW TO REMEMBER BETTER
Table 3 Troubleshooting memory problems: Common memory lapses and strategies to overcome them	
Names	• When you meet someone for the first time, stop and take the time to register his or her name. Many times you may forget a name simply because you didn't notice it being said to you in the first place. • Use a new acquaintance's name in conversation. • Think about whether you like the name. • Think of people you know well who have the same name. • Associate the name with an image, if one comes to mind. For example, link the name Sandy with the image of a beach, and imagine Sandy on the beach. Use as much detail as possible—picture her in a bathing suit, on a beach that's familiar to you. • Write the person's name down in your memory notebook, personal organizer, or address book.
Where you put things	• Always put things you use regularly, such keys and eyeglasses, in the same place. • For other objects, repeat aloud where you put them. • As you put an object down, make a point of looking at the place where you put it. • If you still don't think you'll remember, write down in your memory notebook or personal organizer where you put the object.
What people tell you	• Ask someone to repeat what he or she just said. • Ask the person to speak slowly; that way, you'll be able to concentrate better. • Repeat to yourself what the person said and think about its meaning. • If the information is lengthy or complicated (such as advice from your doctor), record it on your cell phone or a small voice recorder, or take notes.
Appointments	• Write them down in an appointment book, in a calendar that you look at daily, or in your personal organizer.
Things you must do	• Write them down in your personal organizer or calendar. • Write yourself a note and leave it in a place where you'll see it (for instance, on the kitchen table or by the front door). • Ask a friend or relative to remind you. • Put an object associated with the task you must do in a prominent place at home. For example, if you want to order tickets to a play, leave a newspaper ad for the play near your telephone. • If you must do something at a particular time (such as take medicine), set an alarm.

Adapted with permission from Winifred Sachs, Ed.D., Center for Cognitive Remediation and Treatment, Beth Israel Deaconess Medical Center.

electronic organizer or memory notebook. You may want to list the medications you are taking and when to take them; your medical history; names and phone numbers of your doctors, health insurance company, homeowner's insurance, and credit card companies; and work numbers of your closest relatives and friends.

Locations. Keep maps of your area and other places you visit regularly in your car or at home. Before going somewhere new or unfamiliar, check the map. Visualizing where you are going can help reinforce your memory of the verbal directions you may have written down. And just knowing that you have a map can help minimize any anxiety you may feel about getting lost. If you have a GPS in your car, don't become so reliant on it that you don't pay attention to where you're going. Otherwise you'll never memorize the routes.

Checklists. For procedures that you may have difficulty remembering from one time to the next (like using a digital camera or programming your video recorder), write the steps down and post them nearby.

Behavioral strategies
Certain behavioral strategies can help improve your ability to learn new information effectively and retain it over time.

Focus. Your ability to focus your attention and absorb information quickly declines with age and contributes to age-related memory loss. The slowdown in processing causes a bottleneck of information entering your short-term memory, reducing the amount of information that can be acquired and encoded into long-term memory. You can enhance your focus and attention by doing the following:

- When someone is talking to you, look at the person and listen closely. If you missed something that was said, ask the person to repeat it or to speak more slowly.

- Paraphrase what is said to make sure that you understand it and to reinforce the information. For example, if someone says, "We can see the movie either at Loews Theater at 7:30 or at the Paramount at 7:50," you might respond, "Which would you prefer, 7:30 at Loews or 7:50 at the Paramount?"

- If you find that you tend to become distracted during conversations, try getting together with people in quiet environments, such as homes instead of noisy restaurants. When you do meet people at a restaurant, sit at a table near a wall. If your companions sit against the wall and you sit facing them, you'll be able to focus on them without having your attention wander to other diners.

- You can improve your ability to focus on a task and screen out distractions if you do one thing at a time. Try to avoid interruptions. If someone asks you something while you're in the middle of reading or working, ask if the person can wait until you're finished. Don't answer the phone until you've finished what you're doing—let voice mail take the call.

Repeat. You will remember new factual information more effectively if you repeat it to yourself or out loud. If someone gives you directions, for example, repeat them to the person to make sure that you got them right. Discussing newly learned material with a friend or colleague is another way to help reinforce it in your mind.

Ensure comprehension. The more thoroughly you understand new information, the greater the odds that you will remember not only the general concept but also the details. You can improve your comprehension by rereading material, asking questions about it, and discussing it.

Make a note. How many times have you had a brilliant idea while getting ready for bed or standing in line and then forgotten it? Many people assume that if a thought is important enough, they will remember it. But this is unrealistic. When something significant occurs to you, write it down as soon as you can. The act of writing things down actually helps reinforce them in your mind, so you may not even need to refer to your notes to help jog your memory.

Before going to the doctor's office, make a list of questions you want to ask or things you want to mention. Jot down other thoughts as they come to mind: ideas related to your job, possibilities for birthday and holiday presents, the names of restaurants you'd like to try or books you'd like to read, or movies that you didn't see when they were first released. These are the sorts of ideas that often fade with time, but that you know you'll want to remember.

Practice spaced rehearsal. Research on learning has shown that "spaced rehearsal" is more effective than "cramming." In other words, you will remember something more effectively if you rehearse it for one minute once an hour for 10 consecutive hours than if you rehearse it for 10 minutes all at once.

If you have trouble retaining complicated information—for instance, when you read an article, take a course, or start a new project at work—try using spaced rehearsal. Write down the main points of what you have just learned and then review your notes once or twice. Read them again the following day and then again the day after. Spacing out these study sessions gives your brain a chance to consolidate the information that you have learned and form a more durable memory of it. Neuroscientists have found this technique helpful even for people with mild cognitive impairment.

Do small tasks first. It's only natural to turn your attention to the large, important tasks at hand and let the mundane tasks slide. The problem with this approach is that small tasks, like answering phone messages or filling out a form for your child's school photo, tend to pile up and then get forgotten. If you act on them quickly, you don't have to worry about remembering to do them later.

Be patient. One of the main reasons memory declines with age is that the brain processes information more slowly. Give yourself the time you need to absorb new information. Don't consider it a sign of personal failure that you need to slow down in order to learn something new. Experts note that the speed with which you learn new information is just one component of your mental abilities, and it's not even the most important one.

Many older people who participated in the MacArthur Foundation study said that when mental pursuits were important to them, they could compensate for the slowdown in their mental processing by being patient with themselves and working harder.

Memory-enhancing techniques

You've probably heard stories about people with extraordinary memories and wondered how they do it. You may also have heard the term "mnemonics," which comes from Mnemosyne, the Greek goddess of memory, and refers to techniques for remembering information. One mnemonic device is to think of a word that rhymes with a person's name so that you don't forget the name. Another is to come up with a sentence or phrase to help you remember something, such as "Every Good Boy Does Fine" for recalling E, G, B, D, and F, the notes that fall on the lines of the treble-clef musical staff.

Associations

When you learn something new, immediately relate it to something you already know. Making connections is essential for building long-term memories. What you're really doing is making the information meaningful, thus aiding your hippocampus in consolidating it. Making connections between new and old information also takes advantage of the older pattern of synaptic activation, piggybacking the new material onto a prefabricated network.

Remember names by making associations with the first letters. For example, it's fairly easy to remember the National Aeronautics and Space Administration because it is familiar as the acronym NASA. You might try this technique with people's names, too. Let's say you meet someone named Louise Anderson. Her initials are L.A., an association that's easy to remember because it's already familiar as the abbreviation for Los Angeles.

Make associations to remember numbers such as access codes or passwords that you need to use regularly but, for security reasons, don't want to write down and keep in your pocket. For example, if you need to remember the number 221035 to get your voice mail: 22 could remind you of "catch-22," and 10 might be your house number, while 35 was your age when your oldest child was born.

"Chunking" information

Another technique for remembering a long series of items is to regroup them—for example, so that a list of 15 things is organized into three groups of five. For example, when you do grocery shopping, think of the items you need by categories, such as dairy, produce, desserts, frozen foods, and so on.

Chunking is also useful for remembering numbers. Phone numbers are naturally chunked into the area code, local exchange, and remaining four digits. Let's say your checking account number is 379852654. Instead of memorizing it as a string of nine single digits, try grouping the digits into three triple-digit numbers: 379, 852, and 654. That way, you'll reduce the number of chunks of information you need to remember from nine to three.

Method of loci

This technique originated in ancient Greece and it is still one of the best ways to memorize complex or lengthy material, like speeches. The idea is to link the main points of the material to specific locations so that thinking of those locations triggers your recall.

Here's how it works: First, think of a familiar route, such as your commute to work, and imagine traveling that route, noting the stores and other landmarks along the way. Next, pick out the main points in your speech or other information and relate each point in sequence to a landmark on your route. When giving your speech (or recalling the information), think about commuting to work and seeing the landmarks. The image of the landmarks will help you remember the points of your speech. It helps if you vividly picture the images of your route, and also vividly picture something from your speech in that place. For example, if one of the points in your speech deals with a publication your company just put out, picture that publication—the title page just as it looks in real life—on the doorstep of the coffee shop you pass every day.

The loci that you use can also be rooms in your home, which you can imagine walking through sequentially, maybe starting at the front door and walking whatever path you normally take through the house. As you picture your path, mentally drop images from your speech along this route.

The SQ3R Method

SQ3R stands for Survey, Question, Read, Recite, and Review. This five-step method is particularly effective for mastering a large volume of technical information from a textbook or professional document.

Survey the material by reading through it quickly. Concentrate most on the chapter headings and subheadings, as well as the first sentence of each paragraph, to get an overview.

Question yourself about the main points of the text. The more provocative and interesting your questions, the better able you will be to mentally organize the material when you re-read it.

Read the text carefully for comprehension, keeping in mind your questions from the second step. Don't take notes or underline yet—doing so at this stage can actually interfere with your comprehension by interrupting the flow of information.

Recite what you have just read, either to yourself or to someone else. Speaking out loud helps deepen your understanding of the material. Now is also the time to take notes.

Review the text, as well as your notes, a day or two later. Now, think critically about the information: does it support or contradict other information you know about the subject? Go back to your questions from step two. Can you answer them? Do any questions remain? Review the text quickly several more times over the next several days or weeks to help your brain consolidate and store it.

Professional memory training

You can go it alone and teach yourself techniques for strengthening your memory. Or you can get professional memory training. Some medical centers offer memory training

---

Phyllis's story: A patient's experience

"I used to have a sharp memory," says Phyllis, 58. But then Phyllis started having trouble remembering all sorts of things. She'd forget where she left her glasses and her keys at home. She'd forget the details of conversations. Formerly an avid reader, she had trouble retaining information that she'd read.

Her doctor recommended that she see a therapist who specializes in helping people devise strategies and systems to improve everyday memory function. At her first session, the therapist asked Phyllis to tell her specifically what she'd been forgetting, then proposed a strategy for each type of memory lapse. Once a month, Phyllis met with the therapist to discuss how well the strategies were working and to fine-tune them as needed.

For example, the therapist suggested that Phyllis put her glasses and keys in the same places whenever she came home. On the occasions when she had to leave them somewhere else, the therapist told her to say out loud where she was putting them. For example, if the phone rang as she was coming in the door and she rushed into the kitchen to answer it, she would say, "I'm putting my keys on the kitchen table."

To remember information from conversations, the therapist helped Phyllis learn how to paraphrase during the course of the conversation. Restating the information in her own words would reinforce it in her mind.

To improve concentration while reading, the therapist recommended creating a place in her home just for reading that was free of distractions. Phyllis also learned how to make a brief written note summarizing the key aspect of each section of the material she was reading.

Phyllis feels that most of the strategies have proved to be extremely helpful. She still struggles to concentrate on what she's reading, although she's doing better than before she started seeing the therapist. Now that her last memory-coaching session is over, the most encouraging improvements are that she can almost always find her keys and glasses and follow the details of conversations. "I feel my memory is nearly back to normal," she says.

---

programs in which people meet every week or so to learn memory-enhancement techniques, then practice them as homework. Another alternative is to attend a series of individual sessions with a clinician who specializes in memory and other cognitive problems, such as a psychologist, occupational therapist, or speech pathologist. Such a specialist can recommend specific strategies for the types of memory problems that affect you (see "Phyllis's story: A patient's experience," page 39).

Do memory training programs work? Studies on the effectiveness of memory-enhancement programs have found some benefit. A recent study done by researchers at the University of California, Los Angeles, Center on Aging found that older adults improved their memories after a six-week program that included memory training, physical activity (daily walking or swimming), stress reduction, and a healthy diet high in antioxidants. The subjects were 94 people living in retirement communities, with an average age of 81. The researchers tested the participants' memories at the beginning, middle, and end of the study, and found that over all, the people's memories had improved. The subjects also felt their memories were better. An important limitation of the study was that there was no control group to which the researchers compared the subjects who received the memory training and lifestyle intervention.

The four memory techniques used in the study were based on those found in the book *The Memory Bible: An Innovative Strategy For Keeping Your Brain Young* by psychiatrist Gary Small, an author of the study. The techniques were taught sequentially, and participants were expected to practice each skill at home the week it was taught, according to clinical neuropsychologist Karen Miller, the lead author of the study. These are the four techniques they learned:

1. *Look, snap, connect* is all about paying attention, since you can't remember what you don't notice in the first place, and then using visualization to solidify the memory. *Look* refers to slowing down and noticing what you want to remember, such as the fact that you parked your car in section 3B of the parking garage. *Snap* means taking a mental snapshot of the item. That could be a literal image of the parking garage sign, though you'll probably be more likely to remember a more elaborate image, such as that of three bumblebees (representing the 3B section you parked in). *Connect* involves connecting the image and the thing you want to remember—in this case, the three bees and where you parked. So you could imagine the bees in your car. Then when you pause to remember where you parked after coming back to the garage, you'll

likely draw up the image of the three bees buzzing in your car.

2. *The story method*, used by many memory researchers, expands on Look, Snap, Connect. It is helpful when you need to remember many items, such as a list of things to do. In this case, you assign each item a visual image to represent it in the story, and then you make up a story with those images in it. Say you have to buy a present for your wife after work, then get your dog groomed, then pick up your daughter from dance class, and then call your mother in Florida. You might picture a present buckled into the front seat of your car. Then, as you're driving the familiar route to the store, you picture your wet and soapy dog running out in front of the car. Chasing after it is your daughter, dressed in a tutu. Next, a pile of Florida oranges rains down on your car. When you go to remember what to do, you tell yourself the story you created, remembering each errand one by one.

3. *The categorization technique* consists of taking groups of objects and chunking them into categories so you can remember them more easily. For example, if you have a list of items to get at the grocery store, you can remember them in groups such as bread, dairy, fruits, etc. When you get to the store, you can shop for the items one category at a time, since that's how you memorized them.

Can computer brain-training games save your brain?

"The widely held belief that commercially available computerized brain-training programs improve general cognitive function in the wider population in our opinion lacks empirical support. The central question is not whether performance on cognitive tests can be improved by training, but rather, whether those benefits transfer to other untrained tasks or lead to any general improvement in the level of cognitive functioning."

The above quote, from authors of a 2010 article in the journal *Nature,* may disappoint people who have shelled out hundreds of dollars on a computerized brain fitness program in the hopes that it will preserve their intellect. The conclusion stems from their study of 11,430 people between the ages of 18 and 60 who were randomly assigned to one of three online cognitive exercise programs. The first focused on reasoning, planning, and problem solving; the second focused on broader tasks of memory, attention, mathematics, and other skills; and the third (the control) involved searching online for answers to obscure questions. After six weeks, people in the first and second groups boosted their scores on the specifically assigned brain-training games. But they showed no improvement (compared with the control group) when they repeated the more general cognitive testing that had been done at the start.

An earlier study, sponsored by Posit Science, the company that created the popular Brain Fitness Program, used standard memory tests to assess 487 people over age 65, half of whom were assigned to complete the program's 40 hour-long sessions. The other half—the control group—watched educational DVDs and were then quizzed on the material. The software users boosted their memory and attention scores more than the control group. But their self-reported improvement in everyday situations was fairly similar: 48% for the Brain Fitness group versus 40% for the controls.

A newer study used functional magnetic resonance imaging (fMRI) technology to identify brain changes from computer-based memory training games that get harder as the player improves. The subjects were 23 healthy adults with an average age of 64. Twelve people participated in the memory training, and 11 were controls who played a simpler version of the game. As seen in the brain scans, brain activity decreased in a certain part of the cortex of the training group, but not in the controls. The researchers wrote that this suggests that people who got the training increased their "neural efficiency." This means they were able to use a smaller amount of the brain to solve the problems posed by the computer games, and they were able to do it faster.

There are no studies comparing one commercially available program to another or to other mind-bending hobbies. Other factors that make it tricky to assess the worth of any computer program are the potential impact of programs that become more challenging as the player's level of success increases; the effect of the competitive features of a program; and the person's desire to get his or her money's worth from buying the software, some of which costs nearly $400.

Most experts agree that simply playing games that require concentration will not help you remember important names, faces, and appointments. What works are practical tools that are designed to address specific problems you are encountering in your daily life. To stay sharp, your mind needs regular workouts in creative thinking, problem solving, and intellectual focus—all of which are available without spending much money. Look to an activity you enjoy (reading, playing cards, or doing crossword puzzles are some good examples) for your cognitive stretch, or if you're feeling ambitious, learn to speak a foreign language or play a musical instrument.

4. *Face/name association* addresses the common problem of forgetting the name of a new acquaintance. This technique links the name with something prominent about the person's looks. For example, if Carlos has a big nose, you might think of a car parked on his nose. Or if Christine has curly hair, you might think of Christmas ornaments hanging from her curls.

Another study looked at the effects of a broader program on people with mild cognitive impairment. This program encompassed memory skills training and cognitive behavioral therapy, a psychological counseling method that helps people identify and modify negative patterns of thinking. At the end of the program, the participants performed slightly better than a control group on a memory test.

If you are considering a memory-enhancement program, choose one that is run by a health professional with specialized training in cognitive rehabilitation. Beware of memory-enhancement programs that use computer games as a one-size-fits-all means of strengthening your memory (see "Can computer brain-training games save your brain?" at left). People with memory problems that are substantial enough to interfere with their daily lives are most likely to benefit from individual treatment, where their particular needs can be identified and addressed. ▼

When to see a doctor

If you're concerned about your memory, or if people close to you have noticed some worrisome trends, see your doctor for an exam. Because memory loss can be a symptom of many different medical problems, it's important to identify the cause and begin treatment as soon as possible. In some cases, addressing a medical disorder or treating an emotional problem can lead to improvements in memory. For instance, people with depression or sleep disorders often find that treating those conditions improves their memory function or at least prevents further decline. If, on the other hand, you learn that your problem is normal age-related memory loss, you can relax, knowing that there is nothing significant wrong and that simple strategies and lifestyle changes can help strengthen your memory (see "Special Section: Improving everyday memory," page 35).

The first step

Begin with a consultation with your primary care physician. Because this doctor knows you and your medical history, he or she is in a good position to relate your memory symptoms to medications you are taking and medical conditions you have had. But don't necessarily expect to walk out of your doctor's office with a definitive diagnosis. There is no single test that can pinpoint the cause of memory loss. The diagnostic process often requires a physical exam, a variety of tests, and, depending on the results, monitoring over a period of several months or even longer.

Expect your doctor to ask you a lot of questions about your memory. For example:

- How long have you been having problems?
- Did the trouble come on gradually or suddenly?
- What sorts of things have become hard to remember?
- Are your difficulties preventing you from doing ordinary things like cooking or paying the bills?

- Are you taking any prescription or over-the-counter medications?

These questions help the doctor narrow down the possible causes of your memory loss. For example, the doctor will need to know whether you are taking any medications that might have a known association with memory impairment. If your memory loss came on suddenly—and occurred shortly after taking a drug that is known to affect memory—then the diagnostic process may focus on that drug. Depending on the medication, the doctor may ask you to stop taking it or may prescribe a different drug to see whether your memory improves.

Your answers about the nature of your memory loss also provide important clues. If you're having trouble remembering the names of people you meet and you forgot one or two doctors' appointments, that suggests that the problems you're experiencing—however troublesome—probably fall in the normal range. But if your memory difficulties are forcing you to cut back on activities you once did regularly, the underlying cause may be something other than normal aging. Another way to look at the difference between normal memory problems and more troubling ones is whether the episodes are isolated occurrences—a missed appointment here or there, say—or if they are happening more and more often.

Because certain emotional and medical conditions can affect memory, the doctor will review your medical history, ask you about new symptoms and illnesses, perform a physical exam, and may order blood tests. For example, the doctor will measure your blood pressure and blood sugar to look for hypertension or diabetes. If you have one of these conditions, your doctor can make sure that it is properly controlled, either with medication or through lifestyle adjustments, such as a modified diet. Your doctor may also check your blood and urine for signs of kidney or thyroid problems. The doctor may ask whether you've been under a lot of stress lately or if you've been feeling blue, because stress and depression can cause memory impairment as well as loss of interest in previously enjoyable activities. If depression is an issue, your doctor may refer you to a psychologist or a psychiatrist for further evaluation and treatment.

To reach a clear diagnosis, the doctor may need you to track your symptoms for several months, and so may ask you or your spouse to keep a record of your symptoms and then return to the office after that period. He or she can then determine if the symptoms are improving, staying the same, or getting worse.

Neuropsychological testing

If your symptoms warrant a more comprehensive evaluation, your physician may refer you to a neuropsychologist, a doctor who specializes in the relationship between brain and behavior. A neuropsychological examination begins with a thorough review of your history as well as a review of the diagnostic studies and tests that you've already had. Neuropsychologists typically use a battery of paper-and-pencil tests of mental abilities to comprehensively evaluate your cognitive function. The tests assess attention, memory, executive function, language, and spatial ability. The doctor may also use tests or questionnaires to gauge your mood. Not all neuropsychologists use the same tests, but they all look at this same spectrum of mental functions. A technician may help administer the tests.

The neuropsychologist will interpret and analyze the test results in light of your age, level of education, and other variables that influence cognitive ability and memory capacity, as well as in the context of your medical history and other diagnostic studies. That way, he or she can determine if the findings suggest a specific type of disorder or if they reflect normal age-related changes in cognitive function. The following are the kinds of tests that are used. Your doctor will probably refer you to a specialist for additional testing (which may include brain-imaging tests) if your examination and initial test results suggest the possibility of a neurological or medical disorder.

Testing attention

Failure to pay close enough attention is one of the primary reasons people fail to learn new information—they never absorbed it completely in the first place. There are many tests that can be used to assess attention. As one example, the neuropsychologist might read you a sequence of numbers and then have you repeat back as many as you can remember.

Testing memory

Memory testing usually requires that you listen to or view some information and answer questions about it or reproduce it immediately afterward, and then again 10 to 30 minutes later. Some memory tests entail learning and remembering visual information, such as a picture that you are asked to study or a design you are asked to copy. The neuropsychologist might also test your long-term memory by asking you questions about your personal history or factual information you may have learned in the past, comparing it to information gathered from medical records or other sources.

Testing executive function

Executive function is the umbrella term for the high-level mental functions that involve the overall regulation of thought and behavior, such as reasoning, problem solving, planning, initiation, inhibiting impulses, and resisting distraction in order to stay focused on a task. You use such functions even when doing simple things like following a recipe. These abilities often become impaired early in the course of Alzheimer's disease.

One assessment of executive function is the Trail-Making Test. The first phase of this paper-and-pencil test shows circles, each with a number inside it. The test-taker must connect the circles in numerical order. On the second phase there are circles containing either a number or a letter. In this case, the test-taker connects the circles by alternating between the numbers and the letters: 1 to A to 2 to B, and so on. The test is scored according to speed and accuracy.

Executive function is also important in appreciating the subtle, implicit rules that guide social interactions—for example, exhibiting normal consideration for others and the motivation to engage with them. People who are having difficulty in this area are often unaware of the problem; family members may be the first to notice a personality change. These types of problems with executive function are usually not assessed through testing but rather through direct observation and discussion with family members.

Testing language

Language functions include the abilities to express yourself through speaking and writing and to understand what another person is saying or what you are reading. The neuropsychologist may ask you to name common objects or pictured items. Problems with naming and word finding can be early symptoms of Alzheimer's disease. You may be asked to follow instructions as a

Watching the brain at work

Improvements in brain-imaging technology have revolutionized what we know about how the brain remembers and where memories are stored. Magnetic resonance imaging (MRI) and computed tomography (CT) scans can show the shape, size, and contour of the brain and other aspects of internal anatomy. Electroencephalogram (EEG) and event-related potential (ERP) studies allow researchers to precisely track the timing of different memory processes within the brain. Since the 1980s, scientists have been able to trace the activity of the living, working brain with the help of functional imaging techniques such as single-photon emission computed tomography (SPECT), positron emission tomography (PET), and functional magnetic resonance imaging (fMRI). These methods scan blood flow and track the brain's use of certain substances to show which parts of the brain are most active during a particular activity.

MRI scans have revealed key structural differences between the brains of young people and old, and between old people with normal age-related memory loss and those with Alzheimer's disease. These tests have also illustrated that certain brain areas shrink in people with abnormal memory impairment from conditions such as Alzheimer's.

SPECT and PET can help doctors identify regions with abnormally low blood flow or metabolic activity within important brain areas years before shrinkage of those areas is visible on a structural image from MRI. This type of technology also disproved the long-held myth that memories are stored in just one "memory bank" in the brain. Instead, researchers could see diverse areas of the brain become activated as people learned and processed new information, and as they remembered things. Scientists determined that memory relies upon a widely distributed network of interconnected brain regions.

SPECT and PET scanning have become useful in diagnosing Alzheimer's disease because they can reveal abnormal patterns of blood flow or energy metabolism in brain regions that are affected early in the onset of the disease. Once confined to research studies, these tests have now become clinical tools for evaluating patients with cognitive symptoms.

A specific type of PET scan, called FDG-PET, which maps glucose uptake in the brain, has gained wide acceptance as a way to differentiate Alzheimer's disease from normal aging and other dementias. The real promise of FDG-PET, however, may be in the ability to detect Alzheimer's based on reduced glucose metabolism in the brain many years before symptoms appear. This knowledge is vital to the future development of therapies that might halt the disease at a point when cognitive function can be preserved. FDG-PET is one of the imaging techniques explored in the National Institutes of Health's multiyear, multimillion-dollar Alzheimer's Disease Neuroimaging Initiative (ADNI), which began in 2004. One of the studies to come out of the initiative thus far has shown that the FDG-PET results of MCI patients at the start of the study more accurately predicted clinical progression to dementia than two standard neuropsychological tests. This finding, along with greater consistency between PET evaluations, may make it easier to conduct studies on therapies for dementia.

Another potential breakthrough in brain imaging came in January 2011, when the FDA gave conditional approval to an injectable radioactive compound called florbetapir. This compound is proposed for use with PET imaging of beta-amyloid plaque deposits in the brain. The agency said some training needs to be done to make sure the scans are read correctly before it can be given full approval, but that florbetapir-enhanced PET scans do seem to have a place in ruling out Alzheimer's disease. If a person goes to the doctor with changes in memory or thinking, and the scan shows no detectable amyloid buildup in the brain, then Alzheimer's could be ruled out. However, if amyloid proteins show up on the scan, that does not mean as much, since having amyloid buildup in the brain does not definitely mean that a person has Alzheimer's disease.

An important feature of florbetapir is that it can be stored for a relatively long period of time, and therefore can be made off-site. This is different from other compounds, such as PiB (see Figure 7, page 45), that previously have been used to image beta-amyloid plaques in the brain. In the past, only very few research centers could afford to do this testing because they needed to have an extremely expensive machine (called a cyclotron) on-site to mix the compound very soon before the PET study was done.

way of determining if you understand what's being said. You may also be asked to read a brief paragraph, repeat phrases, or describe a picture in writing.

Testing spatial ability

Spatial ability includes analyzing visual information such as shapes, faces, and routes between locations on a map. Because the right side of the brain plays a primary role in analyzing spatial information, people who are having difficulty with this type of function may have a condition that has damaged the right hemisphere, such as a stroke. Although it is relatively uncommon, there is a visual variant of Alzheimer's disease, which begins with symptoms that suggest right-sided or posterior brain dysfunction. Spatial ability tests include drawing and copying designs, solving maze puzzles, and putting blocks together to construct a specific pattern.

Brain-imaging tests

A magnetic resonance imaging (MRI) or computed tomography (CT) scan produces a structural image of your brain (see "Watching the brain at work," page 44). These imaging methods provide the most definitive method of identifying certain causes of memory problems, such as a stroke, brain tumor, hydrocephalus (an enlargement of the ventricles within the brain that contain cerebrospinal fluid), or a subdural hematoma (a collection of blood under the surface of the skull). All of these conditions can injure the brain, producing neurological and cognitive symptoms. Treatment for these conditions is often successful, particularly if they are detected early. ▼

Figure 7 PiB scans to detect Alzheimer's

Pittsburgh Compound B, or PiB, represented a major breakthrough in the diagnosis of Alzheimer's disease and in the evaluation of potential treatments. When PiB is injected into the vein of a patient before he or she has a PET scan, it binds to amyloid deposits in the brain, one of the hallmarks of Alzheimer's disease. The PET scan can then identify the PiB and therefore the location and amount of amyloid deposits. PiB is not approved for use outside of clinical trials.

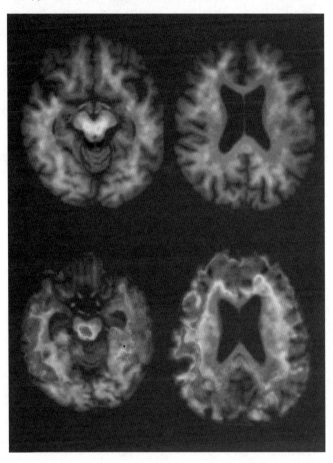

The top picture shows a brain with no amyloid deposits. In the bottom picture, the highlighted areas are where PiB (shown in red) has attached to amyloid deposits. For more detailed, full-color versions of these images, see www.health.harvard.edu/brain-imaging.

Medications for memory impairment

The treatment for memory loss depends on the cause. Sometimes it's as simple as treating an underlying disorder such as diabetes, high cholesterol, depression, or thyroid dysfunction, or discontinuing a medication like diphenhydramine (Benadryl). There is currently no approved prescription medication for treating normal age-related memory loss. And several once-promising drugs and dietary supplements—including ginkgo biloba (see below)—have fallen by the wayside, as more rigorous testing failed to demonstrate clear benefits.

Even the five FDA-approved medications for Alzheimer's disease are not cures, but they are moderately effective in reducing the symptoms of Alzheimer's disease. The benefits are only temporary, however; no drug so far has proved to prevent or reverse the damage done by Alzheimer's.

■ **Cholinesterase inhibitors.** The drugs in this class work by preventing the breakdown of acetylcholine, a neurotransmitter that's important for memory and learning; they are rivastigmine (Exelon), galantamine (formerly Reminyl, renamed Razadyne), donepezil (Aricept), and tacrine (Cognex). All four drugs show similar benefits in treating the symptoms of Alzheimer's disease, but they are only moderately effective, which means they might delay the progression of symptoms by a number of months, though some studies have shown that the drugs can keep symptoms stable for up to three years. This delay in disease progression could possibly enable patients to maintain independence for a longer period, among other benefits. After taking one of them for several weeks, about half of patients are somewhat more alert and better able to care for themselves and engage in activities. A review of 29 studies found that these drugs might also ease some of the psychiatric symptoms of Alzheimer's, such as depression, anxiety, hallucinations, and delusions.

Where the drugs differ is in convenience of use and severity of side effects. Tacrine, the first FDA-approved drug for the treatment of Alzheimer's disease, is rarely prescribed today because it can cause liver damage. The side effects of the other drugs are primarily gastrointestinal symptoms, including nausea and diarrhea. They have also been known to cause slowed heart rate, fainting, vivid dreams, and muscle discomfort. Donepezil, an extended-release formulation of galantamine (Razadyne ER), and the rivastigmine patch are the most convenient of the drugs because they are taken just once a day, whereas

A no-go for memory

Ginkgo biloba, an extract from the nuts and leaves of the maidenhair tree, has been widely touted as a memory booster. Americans and Europeans spend hundreds of millions of dollars a year on ginkgo products. But the popularity of this supplement is more of a testament to the power of marketing than to any measurable brain benefits from ginkgo, according to a large body of research.

Ginkgo biloba has been tested in dozens of studies involving both healthy people and those with mild to severe cognitive impairments, but the findings have been disappointing. For example, in a 2009 report in *The Journal of the American Medical Association*, researchers tested a twice-daily dose of a 120-mg extract of ginkgo biloba or a placebo in more than 3,000 people between the ages of 72 and 96 with normal cognition or mild cognitive impairment. After an average follow-up of just over six years, the researchers found no differences in memory, attention, or other thinking skills between the two groups. A related study found no reduction in the overall rate of developing dementia or Alzheimer's disease in older persons with normal cognition or MCI.

A 2009 review by the Cochrane Collaboration, an international group of independent experts, evaluated 36 studies testing ginkgo biloba in people with cognitive impairment or dementia and concluded the evidence of any benefit for the extract was "inconsistent and unreliable."

standard galantamine and rivastigmine are taken twice a day.

Some physicians also prescribe cholinesterase inhibitors for people with MCI. In 2005, a study published in *The New England Journal of Medicine* showed that people with MCI who took donepezil were less likely to show signs of dementia within a year than people who took either a placebo or vitamin E supplements. Moreover, their neuropsychological test performance tended not to decline over the first 18 months of treatment. However, the benefit was relatively short-lived: after three years, the rate of progression to Alzheimer's was no lower among those who took donepezil than it was among the other groups.

Memantine. Memantine (Namenda) is also FDA-approved for treating moderate to severe Alzheimer's disease. It is an NMDA-receptor antagonist, which blocks glutamate, a neurotransmitter, from attaching to NMDA receptors in the brain. Too much glutamate stimulating these receptors can damage neurons and synapses, leading to memory loss and problems with other brain functions. Like the cholinesterase inhibitors, though, this drug does not prevent the progression of the underlying disease, though it can slow the advancement of symptoms for a little while.

Doctors prescribe memantine alone or in combination with one of the cholinesterase inhibitors for people with moderate to severe Alzheimer's. ◗

Resources

Organizations

Alzheimer's Association

225 N. Michigan Ave., 17th Floor
Chicago, IL 60601
800-272-3900 (toll-free)
www.alz.org

This nonprofit organization supports research on treatments for Alzheimer's disease and provides information and support to families. The association has local chapters throughout the United States.

Dana Foundation

505 5th Ave., 6th Floor
New York, NY 10017
212-223-4040
www.dana.org

The Dana Foundation is a private organization that supports brain research and educates the public about neuroscience through free publications.

National Institute on Aging

Building 31, Room 5C27
31 Center Drive, MSC 2292
Bethesda, MD 20892
301-496-1752
www.nia.nih.gov

This branch of the National Institutes of Health conducts research and publishes information on aging and health.

National Institute of Mental Health

Science Writing, Press, and Dissemination Branch
6001 Executive Blvd., Room 8181, MSC 9663
Bethesda, MD 20892
866-615-6464 (toll-free)
www.nimh.nih.gov

This branch of the National Institutes of Health is a source of information on depression, anxiety, and other mental illnesses that may contribute to memory loss.

National Institute of Neurological Disorders and Stroke

NIH Neurological Institute
P.O. Box 5801
Bethesda, MD 20824
800-352-9424 (toll-free)
www.ninds.nih.gov

This branch of the National Institutes of Health posts information on Alzheimer's disease, mild cognitive impairment, and other neurological disorders on its website, including the latest findings on drug treatments.

Glossary

acetylcholine: A chemical neurotransmitter that [...] in attention, learning, and memory by helpi[...] communicate with each other.

acquisition: The first step in me[...] brain absorbs new info[...]

age-related cognitive decline: The mild loss of memory and speed of information p[...]

amnesia: A condition [...] characterized by an ina[...] to form new [...] or to remember earlier [...]

amygdala: A brain stru[...] hippocampus and othe[...] is vital to emotional ar[...] memories.

axon: A long filament-like projection of a neuron that conducts electrical signals away from the neuron cell body (nucleus) to other cells.

cerebral cortex: The outer layer of gray matter surrounding the cerebrum that carries out all aspects of higher brain function including thought, memory, sensation, and voluntary movement.

cerebrovascular disease: damage to the blood vessels leading to the brain that reduces blood flow to the brain and can cause stroke.

cognitive function: All of the brain mechanisms involved with thinking, reasoning, learning, and remembering.

cognitive reserve: The capacity of the brain to use alternative neural pathways or thinking strategies in response to neurological injury from conditions such as Alzheimer's disease.

consolidation: A key phase in memory formation, in which the brain transforms newly acquired information into long-term memories.

cortisol: A hormone released by the body in response to physical or emotional stress. High levels of cortisol can damage the regions of the brain that are crucial to memory function.

declarative memory: Memory for facts (semantic memory) and for events (episodic memory); also called explicit memory.

dementia: A progressive decline across multiple cognitive domains, resulting in impairment of everyday function.

dendrite: The small branching part of a neuron that receives electrochemical impulses from other neurons and relays them to the body (nucleus) of the neuron.

encoding: A multistage process by which sensation, perception, or thought is transformed into neural representations that can be stored in memory.

[...]**tion:** A group of cognitive activities that [...] erall regulation of thinking and behavior; the higher-order [...] ocesses that enable us to plan, sequence, [...] tain our behavior toward some goal, incorporating [...] edback and making adjustments along the way.

[...] egions located in the front of the brain that play a major role in executive function.

[...] A seahorse-shaped structure situated within [...] system deep in the brain that has a central role in [...] processing.

[...] A network of brain structures crucial for [...] emotions. The hippocampus, one of the structures that [...] the limbic system, is instrumental in memory formation.

magnetic resonance imaging (MRI): A noninvasive diagnostic radiology procedure that uses magnetic fields to form images of the brain and other internal anatomical structures.

mild cognitive impairment (MCI): A condition characterized by the loss of cognitive function—usually memory—that is more severe than is normal for a person's age, but without obvious impairment in activities of daily living.

neuron: A nerve cell, including its axon and dendrites.

neurotransmitter: A chemical substance that relays signals from one neuron to another.

Pittsburgh Compound B (PiB): A substance that binds to amyloid proteins (markers for Alzheimer's disease) that makes them visible in living brains under positron emission tomography (PET) scanning.

positron emission tomography (PET): A nuclear medicine imaging technique that uses differences in energy metabolism in different areas of the body to produce an image of functional processes in the brain or other organs.

procedural memory: The long-term memory of skills and procedures, or "how-to" knowledge. Also called implicit memory.

retrieval: The act of recalling previously learned information; it involves the reactivation of particular nerve cell pathways that encoded a given piece of information.

synapse: The junction between two neurons, across which chemical neurotransmitters carry messages.

white matter: The inner portion of the brain, composed primarily of axons that are surrounded by a myelin sheath that insulates the nerve fibers (and appears white). Messages are sent between different regions of the brain (gray matter) via these nerve fibers.

working memory: A type of short-term memory process that involves temporarily storing and manipulating information.

Harvard Health Publications
HARVARD MEDICAL SCHOOL
Trusted advice for a healthier life

 Receive *HEALTHbeat*, Harvard Health Publications' FREE email newsletter

Go to **www.health.harvard.edu** to subscribe to *HEALTHbeat*. This free, weekly email newsletter brings you health tips, advice, and information on a wide range of topics.

You can also join in discussion with experts from Harvard Health Publications and folks like you on a variety of health topics, medical news, and views by reading the Harvard Health Blog (**www.health.harvard.edu/blog**).

Order this report and other publications from Harvard Medical School

ONLINE   **www.health.harvard.edu**

MAIL   **Belvoir Media Group**
Attn: Harvard Health Publications
P .O. Box 5656
Norwalk, CT 06856-5656

BULK RATES/
LICENSING   **licensing@belvoir.com**

www.health.harvard.edu
877-649-9457 (toll-free)

Other publications from Harvard Medical School

Special Health Reports
Harvard Medical School publishes in-depth reports on a wide range of health topics, including:

Addiction	Eye Disease	Osteoporosis
Alcohol	Foot Care	Positive Psychology
Allergies	Grief and Loss	Prostate Diseases
Alzheimer's Disease	Hair Loss (women's)	Sensitive Gut
Anxiety and Phobias	Hands	Sexuality
Arthritis	Headache	Six-Week Eating Plan
Back Pain	Hearing Loss	Skin Care
Caregivers	Heart Disease	Sleep
Change Made Easy	Heart Disease & Diet	Strength Training
Cholesterol	High Blood Pressure	Stress Management
Core Workout	Immune System	Stroke
Depression	Incontinence	Thyroid Disease
Diabetes	Knees and Hips	Virus
Diabetes & Diet	Living Longer	Vitamins & Minerals
Energy/Fatigue	Living Wills	Weight Loss
Erectile Dysfunction	Memory	Women's Health
Exercise	Neck & Shoulder Pain	Workout Workbook
Exercise Your Joints	Nutrition	

Periodicals
Monthly newsletters and annual publications, including:

Harvard Health Letter	*Harvard Heart Letter*
Harvard Women's Health Watch	*Harvard Mental Health Letter*
Harvard Men's Health Watch	*Prostate Diseases Annual*

ISBN 161401005-6

9 781614 010050

ISBN 978-1-61401-005-0
SV71000

IM12